SOFTWARE MANUAL PRODUCTION SIMPLIFIED

SOFTWARE MANUAL PRODUCTION SIMPLIFIED

Richard Zaneski

PBI

a petrocelli
book

new york   princeton

Copyright © 1982 Petrocelli Books, Inc.
All rights reserved.

Designed by Diane L. Backes
Typesetting by Backes Graphics

Printed in the United States of America
1 2 3 4 5 6 7 8 9 10

Library of Congress Cataloging in Publication Data

Zaneski, Richard.
  Software manual production simplified.

  Includes index.
  1. Electronic data processing documentation.
I. Title.
QA76.9.D6Z26   658.4'038   82-324
ISBN 0-89433-180-9   AACR2

Table of Contents

Preface

Software Manual Production Simplified is a valuable data processing tool that can be used in two ways:

- As a source in developing a documentation program and applying specific ideas in the preparation and maintenance of manuals.
- As a reference guide once the reader acquires the necessary documentation expertise to perform his job.

The information in this book is organized to stress the human side of documentation. It addresses problems that the reader will face in developing manuals, and their proposed solutions. To supply the reader with an insight into those problems, a broad spectrum of information is covered, ranging from the initial concepts developed in a documentation program through the actual printing of a finished manual. Each area of information is explained logically and supplemented with certain techniques that are necessary in avoiding pitfalls.

In your endeavor to apply the procedures in this book to your particular environment, I wish you well. As you grow in this unique area of data processing, you will receive a certain satisfaction seeing your manuals in print. Further, you will feel a sense of pride when someone compliments you on the professional manner in which you produce manuals. When this happens, you will have become part of a fraternity that prides itself in developing well-organized data processing manuals and coordinating every aspect of their evolution.

To assist you in reaching this goal, certain guidelines must be followed in manual development. This instructional data as well as other areas of information are modularized, a technique I've found helpful in preparing manuals. In addition, this book has been written in such a manner as to reflect the structure of a typical manual, utilizing a numbering scheme necessary for quick reference.

To develop the proper thinking that should be used in evaluating your documentation problem, I've written this book simply, showing how all phases of manual development evolve from management's initial philosophy. Where it's feasible, I lead you through each procedure step-by-step and provide detailed explanations where necessary. In addition, most narratives involving specific types of publications are supported with examples. For the most part, the book follows a certain logical flow. Each area of information fits into the normal sequence of events as follows:

CHAPTER 1–THE RESULTS OF A DOCUMENTATION PHILOSOPHY. This chapter emphasizes the need for a certain philosophy, one that must be developed if management is serious about its documentation problem. It touches on the manner in which documentation has been approached and the ensuing results.

CHAPTER 2–CREATING A DOCUMENTATION POLICY. A documentation policy must be established. To achieve this goal, it is necessary to determine certain guidelines. In addition, the conditions that underlie these guidelines must be established. To this end, specific questions will be discussed. They pertain to the following areas: the type of audiences reading your manuals, types of manuals to be developed, types of approaches in writing, staff and physical requirements, and the necessary production effort. Each area of information forms one aspect of your policy that must be developed to form an organized and well-defined documentation program.

CHAPTER 3–THE DEVELOPMENT OF MANUAL STANDARDS. After establishing an effective documentation policy, a set of workable standards must be established. They will become part of your policy, forming the basic framework of each manual. This chapter, therefore, will instruct the reader in those areas of standards that are critical in any documentation program: the life cycle of a manual and detailed standards necessary in manual development. Their continuous application will provide a firm base from which technical material can be described in an easy and consistent manner.

CHAPTER 4–ACCESSING DATA SOURCES. Once the basic framework of a manual has been established, sufficient data must be gathered with which to work. Several methods of performing this task are explained in this chapter:

1. Studying the requirements analysis, basic project plan, functional specifications, and system specifications.
2. Examining additional written or printed technical material.
3. Interviewing members of the technical staff.
4. Gaining "hands-on" experience with software packages and associated equipment.

In addition, the extent of manual coverage is discussed. After information has been gathered by one or more of the aforementioned methods, it must be studied, sorted, and reduced to the required level of explanation for the benefit of the user.

CHAPTER 5–MANUAL PREPARATION. Once information for a system is formalized, it is incorporated into a manual. As such, it plays a key role in the system's operation on a daily basis. Therefore, it must be geared for its own unique audience and be presented clearly, accurately, and in the simplest possible manner. To assist you, this chapter will probe all the essential writing techniques used in preparing technical, user, installation, and procedure manuals that form the main part of the documentation effort.

CHAPTER 6–THE REVIEW CYCLE. To perform an adequate job of reviewing drafts, a sufficient amount of time must be spent using an effective review procedure which is discussed in this chapter. As an integral part of the review cycle, techniques of proofreading are discussed.

CHAPTER 7–MANUAL MAINTENANCE. After any manual is used over a period of time, it may be necessary to change some areas of information because of improvements, deletions, or a complete revision. The individual maintenance functions are detailed in this chapter. They provide a smooth means of changing the designated areas in the most efficient manner.

CHAPTER 8–ARTWORK AND GRAPHICS IN MANUALS. The most pertinent aspects of graphics, art, and their application to a manual are discussed. This includes related phases of typesetting that are essential in the production of an aesthetically pleasing written product. In addition, the writer's relationship with the artist will be studied.

CHAPTER 9–THE WRITER/PRINTER RELATIONSHIP. Often, the writer may have to deal with printers and vendors to produce a manual. If so, it is necessary to understand certain aspects of this unique area of the writing craft:

1. Knowing the types of printers available.
2. Finding a printer.
3. Determining a printer's capabilities and making a selection.
4. Receiving estimates on a job.
5. Preparing final copy for the printer.
6. Assessing a printer on a short and long term basis.
7. The final printing process.
8. Binding alternatives.

The information in these chapters will show you what's involved in producing a manual, support you in your task, and assist you in developing your own approach. It is essential that you perform your job with an open mind and try to use the techniques I've presented and, possibly, improve them. With time, I'm sure you'll develop an effective program based on management's documentation philosophy. If this philosophy is sound, the final results will be well-organized manuals and a viable method of producing them.

CHAPTER ONE

The Results of a Documentation Philosophy

Software documentation is no longer a second-class citizen; it has emerged as a vital and respectable member of the data processing family. Its importance is slowly being recognized with the continuing development of new and sophisticated software. Yet poor documentation still exists in many quarters, spawned by an ignorance of the writing discipline and sheer complacency. Often, documentation is put aside until the last possible moment. Then, because of the time factor, writing is rushed and an inadequate manual produced. This lack of planning has caused more anguish for data processing managers than the most intricate computer programs and systems.

If this is so, why has senior management not done anything about it? Something *has* been done with satisfying results in publications from several of the larger companies. Because of their resources, talented people were hired, the best approaches in presenting documentation studied, and the best in typesetting and graphics equipment used. This was a major step toward publishing successful manuals and related technical material.

Within the hierarchy of these companies, concern caused the evolution of a documentation philosophy to implement them. To reach this initial stage in its documentation program, management directed its efforts in defining certain concepts which are pertinent in developing a documentation philosophy in today's data processing environment. They are:

- *Basic documentation issues.* Based on the software involved, the following issues were determined.

  —What software products had to be documented?
  —Why was it necessary to document these particular software products?

—Would the resulting documentation be used for internal or external use?

—What aspects of a particular software product or related functions were to be emphasized?

—To what extent was a particular software product or related functions to be explained?

- *Direction to take for the resolution of these issues.* A determination was made as to how the basic documentation issues were to be resolved. It depended on the selection of an individual who could address these issues swiftly and in a professional manner. It required a frank dialogue with key people in the company hierarchy who could provide assistance in giving information and establishing their documentation viewpoints.

- *The meaning of well-organized and documented manuals.* The impact of carefully planned and prepared manuals was considered. As such, two vital questions were asked.

—How would this manual affect the company's business? In the data processing community, *support* is the key to the sale of any successful software product. As part of this support effort, a complete documentation package is necessary. It plays a major role in maintaining a smooth business relationship between a company and its customer.

—How would this manual affect the company in a professional sense? Consideration was given to the professional attitude necessary in producing well-written publications. A successful documentation effort would only be successful if the person in charge had the necessary zeal and drive. His positive approach to the documentation problem would have a tremendous effect on the professional appearance of the company in the documentation area.

- *The most cost-effective means to realize documentation objectives.* The end result of a concentrated documentation program was to be complete and well-organized manuals that would satisfy customers' requirements. With this prime objective in mind, a sufficient amount of money had to be directed toward this effort. Here again, the input of a professional in the documentation area was required, someone who had a firm idea of budget, personnel, and equipment considerations. His expertise in these areas provided the savings required by the company without sacrificing quality in the written product.

By addressing these initial concepts methodically, management was able to develop a documentation philosophy, one which provided stability and direction. In turn, the way was opened for the development of specific policies and the functional ideas to supplement them. However, what happened to those large companies which were too engrossed in other data processing matters to worry about documentation and its impact on the market place? Also, what about the small and medium-sized companies, particularly the numerous software companies that have become part of a burgeoning industry? The answer to these questions is quite simple. Documentation, an area of data processing that could create an impact on efficiency and sales, became a low priority item.

Let's be optimistic, however, and say that your company is concerned about its documentation problem and wants to do something about it. A directive is forwarded to you, as the responsible person, to establish a new image, creating manuals and related materials that are well-organized, technically accurate, and aesthetically pleasing. The initial concern has been shown by management. The basic concepts have been studied and defined, and a documentation philosophy formulated based on a sound understanding of the manual effort. Your task is to help management establish a documentation policy and manual standards. It sounds like an almost impossible task, but through hard work and perseverance, success will be realized.

This type of approach should be taken in today's data processing environment. Once a documentation philosophy is developed, it acts as the cornerstone for the entire documentation program. It supports all phases of manual development, as long as the initial concepts created by management have been addressed and acted upon.

CHAPTER TWO

Creating a
Documentation Policy

To successfully implement a documentation effort of any size, it is necessary to establish a plan, one that requires a definition of certain information. From this information, specific criteria can be developed to formulate a basic documentation policy. As it is gradually brought into practice, this policy sets the tone for present and future publication efforts.

To develop your basic documentation policy, the following questions must first be answered:

- What audiences will read the different types of manuals?
- What types of manuals must be developed?
- What approach should be used to write each type of manual?
- What are the staff and equipment requirements for a documentation effort?
- What production effort should be given the final manuals for maximum effect?

These questions address the main areas with which you must be concerned. To provide assistance in finding answers, these questions are studied in detail in sections 2.1 through 2.5.

2.1   WHAT AUDIENCES WILL READ THE DIFFERENT TYPES OF MANUALS?

Initially the types of audiences for which you will be writing must be identified. This is particularly important in establishing a documentation program. Every manual or related publication must be written with specific users in mind at all times. In the data processing community, for example, your audiences could range from data processing managers to computer room operators. In many instances, users are found outside the data processing environment. When this occurs, the needs of each type of user must be considered and judgments made on the appropriate level of writing.

In your own mind, understand the various types of audiences with which you will be concerned. To do this, study the people involved, develop an insight into their needs, be familiar with their expertise, learn the terminology peculiar to their environment, and discover their documentation weaknesses.

At times, the different audiences may overlap for different types of manuals. Naturally this may cause a problem. For which audiences, therefore, would you address your particular publication? To answer this question, consider a group composed of managers, systems analysts, and non-DP staff members for whom you are writing a manual. *The documentation should be geared for those users having the least data processing knowledge*, in this case the non-DP staff members. Even though the manager or systems analysts might feel the material is too simple, your obligation is to enlighten the less knowledgeable people first. By directing your manual to the non-DP staff members, you still reach all three audiences but in a simpler writing style.

2.2 WHAT TYPES OF MANUALS MUST BE DEVELOPED?

Once the various audiences are known, manuals which they will use must be identified. Normally manuals will fit into one of the following categories:

- *Technical manuals.* Define all technical data necessary for a system's successful programming and implementation.
- *User manuals.* Provide step-by-step instructions in the use of a system product or a certain aspect of that product.
- *Installation manuals.* Provide all technical information and coding necessary to install a software product at a customer's site.
- *Procedure manuals.* Provide instructional information for personnel to perform specific functions in business and data processing environments.

The preparation of each manual is discussed in Chapter 5.

Each category is unique. Together they cover the entire spectrum of data processing, with few exceptions. Of course, specialized categories of manuals could be established, such as training manuals, or manuals that are marketing- and sales-oriented. These require a special expertise and are not discussed in this book. They do, however, play an important role in the dissemination of data processing information.

In determining the types of manuals that are required, consider the four basic categories. You will be concerned with each of them in some form as your experience grows in the writing field.

2.3 WHAT APPROACH SHOULD BE USED TO WRITE EACH TYPE OF MANUAL?

The writing approach taken by a writer will affect his or her working life until a particular job is complete. Therefore, careful consideration must be given to the manner in which the actual task of writing is done. Past experience has shown that a writer can perform the technical writing function in three ways:

- *Normally all technical data is gathered by the writer.* He or she can sift through it, organize it, and do the actual writing. Information can be gathered by:
  - Studying the requirements analysis, basic project plan, functional specifications and system specifications.
  - Examining additional written or printed technical material.
  - Interviewing members of the technical staff.
  - Gaining hands-on experience with software packages and associated equipment.

  The techniques (described in Sections 4.1 through 4.4) can be applied assuming the writer has sufficient time to perform the job. If, however, the writer is not proficient with the existing technical data and requires study, time will be lost. To eliminate this problem, management must allow some time consideration in writing a manual. Working with sufficient time and without constant supervision will produce a more precisely written product.

- *Members of the technical staff can do the actual writing of rough drafts based on the writer's original outline and specifications.* Each draft is edited by the writer who ensures that it fits the established standards. This technique is usually faster because the pressure is taken off the writer to some degree. However, the writer must be careful not to entrust the completion of a manual to staff members without careful examination of the data. Too often, gaps of information may occur that have been overlooked by the technical staff. In the final analysis, it is the writer's responsibility for the manual to be correct in every way. Here again, sufficient time must be allocated for the writer to edit the material more carefully.

- *The writer can work through a review committee, acting as a coordinator of information.* All the actual writing is done by members of the technical staff, who are assigned their jobs by the chairman of the committee. In turn, they do the actual writing based on the writer's original outline and specifications. Then they forward their work to the writer, who keeps track of its completion and edits the text. Every draft in the development of a manual must be reviewed by the committee regularly. However, it is the responsibility of the writer to prepare the approved review drafts, ensuring that they conform to the established standards. The completeness and correctness of these drafts are a reflection of the time allotted the writer to finish his or her work.

Needless to say, this technique is extremely time-consuming and is subject to delays because of staff work commitments. The writer must be after individual members constantly to get the work done; however, working with various members of the technical staff gives the writer a broad view of the subject being documented. The end result is a detailed manual.

2.4   WHAT ARE THE STAFF AND EQUIPMENT REQUIREMENTS FOR A DOCUMENTATION EFFORT?

Inevitably the question of staff and physical requirements must be faced. The best time to answer this is in the early part of your planning.

No matter how you avoid it, manpower and budget must be considered. Like any area of business today, our sector of data processing requires an examination of its basic physical needs. How manpower and physical requirements are regarded now will probably affect your documentation effort for as long as it exists at your company.

Initially consider the size of the staff necessary to perform the upcoming work. Naturally if you have determined the type of approach to be used in writing and know the number of projects, you should know immediately how many additional writers are required.

After determining the number of writers necessary to staff the documentation effort, consideration must be given to a supporting staff. Ideally a clerk and typing support would do. Normally a clerk-typist will suffice for a small operation. This function is necessary for the following reasons:

- To keep track of all copies of drafts prepared by the writing staff and all associated sign-off sheets.
- To keep track of all final reproduction used by the printer to produce the final copies of your publication.
- To provide assistance in proofreading.
- To act as an intermediary between the writing staff and art department (if one is available in your company).
- To lessen the work load of the writing staff by allowing it more time for creative work.
- To provide typing or word processing support as the need arises.

The foregoing is a very optimistic view; economics always hinders manpower acquisitions. More than likely, you probably will have to do most of the work yourself, with some typing or word processing support. If you are a manager with many projects, then a problem exists. If, however, one or two technical writers can be hired to assist you, your problem may be resolved.

In addition, if you can obtain a production coordinator, a great deal of the pressure of dealing with printers and vendors will be eliminated. If this is not possible, the writer/printer relationship described in Chapter 9 should be studied.

Besides staff requirements, a writer needs basic physical items to work effectively, such as:

- *An electric typewriter or word processing system.* Either gives you flexibility in preparing draft copies, thereby saving valuable time. In addition, a printed draft provides a clearer picture of the information, particularly when it is printed in a double-spaced format.
- *Storage cabinets with locks.* These storage facilities keep all draft copies, related notes, sign-off sheets and final reproduction in one central area. Thus, your final reproduction can be retrieved when changes are necessary. It also allows you to refer to draft copies of a manual and sign-off sheets when any question arises.
- *Ample storage space for the final printed copies of publications.* It is necessary to have storage space for all manuals and related materials that eventually will be produced. As time goes by and the quality of your work improves, more and more of your manuals will be needed. Therefore, plan for as much storage space as possible. Ideally the storage and inventory of manuals should be assigned to the department responsible for their shipment to customers.

Obviously, staff and physical resources will affect the manner in which a documentation problem is approached. Therefore, define your requirements after a complete analysis of the problems facing you, and present them to management.

2.5   WHAT PRODUCTION EFFORT SHOULD BE GIVEN THE FINAL MANUALS FOR MAXIMUM EFFECT?

The final reproduction effort must be considered. A decision must be made as to the amount of time, work and money to be put into the final packaging of your manuals. *The physical appearance of any written material is vital to its success.* This means the proper use of artwork, color and typesetting. Effective use of this combination creates a positive first impression on a customer or user. This is true even when the manual is used in-house. If this is the type of professional touch you want to introduce in your manuals, you will be successful.

In addition, printing costs should not be disregarded. By carefully comparing estimates and using the best and most dependable printers, a high standard can be achieved in the established timeframe for the right price.

After careful analysis and research, the answers to the five questions outlined in Sections 2.1 through 2.5 will have a profound effect on the way you manage your documentation effort. They will define your basic documentation policy. However, to be effective, the policy must be implemented with a complete set of manual standards.

CHAPTER THREE

The Development of
Manual Standards

A firm documentation policy is not possible without manual standards to provide the consistency and structure vital to the production of successful technical publications. Therefore, it is imperative that these standards encompass all possible conditions that affect the preparation of different types of manuals. Once standards are developed, their application must be pursued on a continuing basis. This is essential for any documentation policy to be effective.

As manuals are a vibrant part of the data processing function, each type has a "life cycle" with distinct phases that must be defined. In turn, aspects of each phase must be clearly shown. To support this life cycle definition, detailed standards must be established which affect the basic manual structure.

The entire standard development function must be initiated by you and submitted to a committee for study and final approval. This committee should be composed of staff members who have an interest in clearly organized and well-written manuals. They should perform their duties knowing that the end result will strengthen their company's documentation policy, making their data processing lives and those of their users easier. To assist the committee in developing standards, explanations of the manual life cycle and detailed standards are provided in sections 3.1 and 3.2.

Early in manual development, each subphase in the life cycle must be assigned certain dates in which specific functions are to begin and be completed. These dates can be written down in a standard listing of phases and subphases as shown in Figure 3-1.

_____ MANUAL

		EST BEG DATE	EST COMP DATE	ACTUAL BEG DATE	ACTUAL COMP DATE
	Outline				
	Data Gathering				
	Data Organization				
P	Chapter 1				
H	Chapter 2				
A	Chapter 3				
S	Chapter 4				
E	Chapter 5				
	Preliminary Artwork				
1	Chapter 1				
	Chapter 2				
	Chapter 3				
	Chapter 4				
	Chapter 5				

	Writing				
P	Chapter 1				
H	Chapter 2				
A	Chapter 3				
S	Chapter 4				
E	Chapter 5				
2	Draft Review				

	Typesetting				
P	Chapter 1				
H	Chapter 2				
A	Chapter 3				
S	Chapter 4				
E	Chapter 5				
3	First Draft Review				

FIGURE 3-1. Standard Life Cycle Listing

	Final Review				
P	Verification				
H	Pagination				
A					
S	Prep. of Front Tables				
E	Prep. of Index				
4	Verification of Front Tables and Index				
	PHASE 5—Printing				

FIGURE 3-1. (continued)

3.1 LIFE CYCLE OF MANUALS

The phases in the life cycle of a manual are:

- Initial preparation and organization.
- Writing and draft reviews.
- Typesetting and typeset draft review.
- Final writer verification.
- Printing.

3.1.1 Phase 1—Initial Preparation and Organization

Phase 1 of the life cycle of a manual consists of four parts:

- The outline.
- Data gathering.
- Data organization.
- Preliminary artwork.

Each part of Phase 1 represents a key element in a manual's life cycle. As such, they should be given prominence in your work schedule. The development of raw data gives you a semblance of order and a precise plan with which to work. Also, the early preparation of artwork allows you to concentrate on writing the manual and rids you of problems connected with its later development.

THE OUTLINE

No matter what type of manual is written, *an outline must be prepared*. Without it, you will be in serious trouble. An outline acts as a road map and serves you well, so long as it is detailed and well-constructed. To this end, an outline must show each chapter of a manual with its sections and subsections. In addition, all tables and illustrations should be listed in numerical sequence as they appear in the manual.

There are no set rules in preparing an outline. As long as all categories of information are covered in the proper order with possibly a brief chapter synopsis, your outline will suffice. However, ensure that the blocks of descriptive information follow a logical sequence from beginning to end. A certain continuity must be established and maintained.

To show you how this continuity is established, study the example shown in Figure 3-2. For purposes of simplicity, general chapter and section headings are used. In addition, the numbering of each section follows the detailed standards that are shown in Subsection 3.2.2.

This simplified outline provides a good starting point for a manual. Bear in mind that your end result may deviate from this example as more detail may be required. In any case, this part of Phase 1 of the manual's life cycle represents the foundation of any documentation project you start. The project's success can be achieved only through the development of a comprehensive outline.

DATA GATHERING

This part of Phase 1 requires a clear understanding of the types of data that are available and how they can be accessed. In addition, there must be a method established to determine the extent of a manual's coverage based on the user's needs. Because of the significance of this aspect of Phase 1, Chapter 4 is devoted to its full explanation.

DATA ORGANIZATION

Once all data has been gathered and a determination made of the extent of a manual's coverage, categorize it by those chapters planned in your outline. Using a basic filing system, ensure that all information for each chapter is broken into its respective sections and subsec-

---

PROPOSED OUTLINE FOR THE XXXXXXX
SYSTEM USER MANUAL

CHAPTER 1—INTRODUCTION
—Discusses the basic philosophy of the manual (i.e., how the manual will help the user) and outlines any special considerations.

1.1 Manual Organization

—Provides a cursory analysis of each chapter to acquaint the user with the contents of the manual.

CHAPTER 2—SYSTEM OVERVIEW
—Reviews the processing cycle of the system and its inter-relationship with any other system from beginning to end. A flow chart is included to supplement the text.

CHAPTER 3—PREPARING CARD INPUT
—Describes the card input prepared for the system in tabular format. All peculiarities will be indicated. Examples will be shown.

3.1 ABC card type
3.2 DEF card type
3.3 GHI card type
3.4 JKL card type
3.5 Coding typical data for input

CHAPTER 4—OUTPUT REPORTS
—Describes the purpose of each report and the output generated by the system (i.e., each field on the report with a report example.)

4.1 Audit report
4.2 Debit report

FIGURE 3-2. Outline Example

CHAPTER 5—ERROR MESSAGES
—Describes all error messages, their meanings, system action, and user action (if any) in tabular format.

*APPENDIX A—TECHNICAL CALCULATIONS AND
                FORMULAS*
APPENDIX B—SYSTEM GUIDELINES
GLOSSARY OF TERMS
INDEX

FIGURE 3-2. (continued)

tions. This includes all rough artwork and tables that fit into the text. Each table and piece of artwork must be identified by number as indicated in the outline. Standards for the different numbering schemes are shown in Subsection 3.2.2.

When you are through compiling all data, verifying its accuracy, and organizing it into its appropriate position within your filing system, this portion of Phase 1 is complete.

PRELIMINARY ARTWORK

It is important in the initial stages of manual development that the rough artwork be completed as soon as possible. When done, the rough artwork should be submitted to the art department (if there is one) or given to an outside artist for preparation. This includes all flow charts, photographs for use in the manual, input forms, output reports, and other miscellaneous items. Bear in mind that it takes a great deal of time to prepare artwork properly. This time will be multiplied greatly if many pieces exist. Therefore, the sooner you assemble the artwork and prepare it, the less you need to worry. If, however, you wait until a manual is near completion, problems in your time schedule will appear.

NOTE: As you extract the rough artwork from your notes, ensure an indication is made that the particular piece of artwork exists. It could possibly be skipped at a later date.

3.1.2 Phase 2—Writing and Draft Reviews

Now that you have formalized an outline, gathered and organized the necessary information, and started preparations on the artwork, the actual writing can be initiated.

When writing a manual or any other data processing publication, continuity must be maintained between chapters. Within each chapter, a physical flow of information must be present between sections and subsections. If the initial preparation of an outline was done correctly, there should be no problem establishing the necessary continuity.

Each manual, of course, must be written based on a set of detailed standards. These standards should be used as the guide for every manual that is produced. The particular set of standards I propose allows a user to access information more easily from a manual. In addition, the documentation can be maintained more efficiently. These two points, ease of access and maintenance, are important to the writer and user so far as time and manpower are concerned. They provide an organized approach to the documentation problem and fulfill the needs of the user by establishing meaningful manuals.

After writing portions of the manual, ensuring that your standards are applied, have the initial rough draft typed. This initial rough draft must be double-spaced to allow for corrections. In addition, insert the rough artwork in the appropriate areas to give the reviewer an idea of how the manual will look.

When the initial rough draft is complete, submit copies to the staff for review. While the draft copies are being reviewed, study the manual yourself to ensure that the following points are covered.

- The manual follows the outline.
- A physical flow of information and continuity is maintained.
- The manual adheres to the standards that have been established.
- No typographical errors, misspellings, or misuses of grammar exist.

At this point, all staff comments should be collected by you and entered in red on a master copy of the initial draft, in addition to any comments by yourself. This draft should be as clear as possible for the typist. *The clearer the copy submitted to the typist, the fewer mistakes will be made and, conceivably, the quicker you will receive the completed draft.* Remember, a faster turnaround gives you more time which can be applied to your work schedule.

On the initial rough draft, explain everything that might be questionable. For example, indicate whether certain sentences must be highlighted or any of the text is to be indented. A full explanation of your requirements will save time. Prior to submitting the initial rough draft for typing, it is a good idea to give the typist a set of standards in which all your requirements are explained.

The initial rough draft review is then followed by a working draft review. In turn, after comments are entered, it is followed by a preliminary draft review. Each review brings the manual closer to type-setting, ensuring it is as technically correct as possible. Of course, each draft follows the same review procedure. Once the preliminary draft has been reviewed and corrected, the manual is ready for typesetting.

3.1.3 Phase 3—Typesetting and Typeset Draft Review

The art department must be informed well in advance as to when the preliminary draft will be received. This notice will give the typesetter enough time to complete whatever work must be done and have it fit into his work schedule. Further, it is essential that your planning schedule and his coincide.

On a predetermined date, submit your preliminary draft to the art department with as much explanation as possible. As discussed earlier, a clear set of detailed standards should accompany a well-typed preliminary draft.

NOTE: All preliminary artwork should have been submitted to the art department during Phase 1—Initial Preparation and Organization.

In addition to a predetermined date of delivery for the typed preliminary draft, know the exact date when you can expect the type-set copy. This is important for your planning. After a copy of the typeset copy is received, the material must be inspected by you and select members of management. At this point, additional data should not be entered because of the typesetting costs involved. If it is impossible to avoid this issue, ensure it is done with management's approval. If editorial changes and vital technical data must be entered, the master copy should be submitted to the art department for revision.

3.1.4 Phase 4—Final Writer Verification

Phase 4 of the life cycle of a manual consists of two critical areas: Final review and pagination of the manual and preparation of the front tables and index.

FINAL REVIEW

This function is necessary on your part to ensure that all re-viewer comments of a vital nature and your editorial comments were entered in the typeset copy. In addition, the organization of the manual, content, and flow of information must be examined again to ensure it meets all criteria. As near a perfect manual as possible must be achieved. Even then, you are not done. Precise proofreading must follow. It is essential in order to avoid any complications at a later date.

PAGINATION AND PREPARATION OF THE FRONT TABLES AND INDEX

Each page must be numbered based on your standards. After all pages are numbered, the table of contents, list of illustrations, and list of tables in the front portion of the manual can be prepared, as well as the title page and any other material preliminary to the actual text of the manual.

Finally the index can be started. Indexing is a unique feature of writing that fulfills a basic need of users. A good index that is cross-referenced gives them the ability to reference a specific topic quickly. Often, time is critical, a luxury which most users do not have. Techniques useful in preparing an index are shown in Subsection 5.1.12.

3.1.5 Phase 5–Printing

After the final draft of a manual has been approved and all corrections entered, arrangements must be made to have it printed. If you are not fortunate to have a production coordinator handle all the printing details, you must take care of the matter yourself.

To process the final reproduction, the following steps must be taken:

- Determine the number of manuals to be printed and stored.
- Have estimates made by several printers.
- Present these estimates to management for approval with a recommendation.
- Submit the final reproduction to the printer and ensure that the printing process follows the predetermined time cycle.

All of these steps are discussed in Chapter 9.

After receiving the correct number of copies from the printer, verify the quality of the work. It is the writer's responsibility to ensure that the manuals are inspected critically. If printing errors or shoddy workmanship is apparent, let the printer know, and demand compensation or satisfaction.

NOTE: Ensure that all final reproduction the printer used is returned in good shape. Place it in a heavy envelope, seal it, identify it as final reproduction, and store it in a locked cabinet for future use.

3.2   DETAILED MANUAL STANDARDS

To prepare a manual, a writer needs a detailed set of standards to follow. Standards are necessary in order to maintain consistency from manual to manual. They provide the cohesion that binds the technical material into a standard format, one that provides ease of access and maintenance.

Standards that are vital in manual development are divided into the following specific categories:

- Manual organization.
- Numbering scheme.
- Manual layout.
- Figure and table titles.
- Artwork reductions and type size.
- Updating of manuals.
- Use of notes.

It is recommended that this information be used as a guide for you to develop your own set of standards. Therefore, study each category and see how each can be applied to your particular data processing environment.

3.2.1 Manual Organization

A manual consists of certain basic areas of information. Their sequential appearance in a manual is:

1. Cover page (front).
2. Title page.
3. Copyright and version number page (if necessary).
4. Table of contents, list of illustrations, and list of tables.

5. Specific chapters (which may consist of sections and, if necessary, subsections).
6. Appendices (if necessary).
7. Glossary (if necessary).
8. Index (if desired).
9. Readers comments page (if necessary).
10. Cover page (back).

Each basic area of information must adhere to specific guidelines.

COVER PAGE

A cover is used for the front and back of a manual. Two types of covers may be used based on a company's requirements:

- The cover may consist of a heavy card stock with suitable printing that identifies the manual and company, in addition to any desired graphic design. Publications using this type of cover page are stapled in two spots on the left-hand side or suitably bound (saddle-stitching or a soluble glue covering along the spine). In addition, the cover page and manual must be three-hole punched to allow the manual's insertion into a binder used for storing small publications.
- If a larger publication is written, it may be necessary to use an adequate three-hole binder that has the title of the manual and company name on its front cover. The cost of the binder will dictate the type of cover used and any associated graphic design.

If a three-hole binder is used, dividers should separate each section of the manual, identifying each chapter, appendix, glossary and index. The divider tabs should be covered with plastic to protect the printed identification from wear.

TITLE PAGE

The title page is the first page of the manual. In the center of the page, the manual will be identified according to your standards, with all capital letters. For example:

```
THE XXXXXXXX SYSTEM
TECHNICAL MANUAL
```

COPYRIGHT AND VERSION NUMBER PAGE

This optional page is on the reverse side of the title page, and is also governed by standards. For instance, the version number (as determined by the company's management and technical staff) will be printed in the center of the page in upper and lower case letters. In addition, a copyright statement will be printed no lower than three-fourths inch from the bottom of the page. Thus:

Copyright 1982 by (name of company). Printed in the United States of America. All Rights Reserved. No part of this manual may be reproduced in any form without the prior written consent of (name of company).

NOTE: Refer to your company's legal staff for the legal requirements necessary to copyright a publication.

TABLE OF CONTENTS, LIST OF ILLUSTRATIONS, AND LIST OF TABLES

The table of contents identifies each chapter, section, and subsection by number and title with its appropriate page. It will be identified by the words "TABLE OF CONTENTS" on top of the page in the center, one inch from the top. In capital letters, succeeding pages of the table of contents will have "TABLE OF CONTENTS" in the small position. Observe the indentation and specific column headings ("Chapter" and "Page" in upper and lowercase letters) shown in Figure 3-3.

TABLE OF CONTENTS

Chapter		Page
1	INTRODUCTION.	1–1
	1.1 Manual Organization.	1–1
2	SYSTEM OVERVIEW	2–1
3	DATA INPUT TO SYSTEM.	3–1
	3.1 ABC Card Type.	3–2
	3.1.1 Card Requirements.	3–3
	3.2 DEF Card Type.	3–4
	3.2.1 Card Requirements.	3–5

FIGURE 3-3. Table of Contents Example

The list of illustrations identifies each figure in the manual by sequential number and title with its appropriate page. It will be identified, for example, by the phrase, "LIST OF ILLUSTRATIONS" on top of the page in the center, one inch from the top in capital letters. Succeeding pages of the list of illustrations will have "LIST OF ILLUSTRATIONS (CONT.)" centered one inch from the top of the page. Observe the specific column headings ("Figure," "Title," and "Page" in upper and lowercase letters) shown in Figure 3-4.

The list of tables identifies each table in the manual by number and title with its appropriate page. It will be identified, for example, by the words "LIST OF TABLES" on top of the page in the center, one inch from the top in capital letters. Succeeding pages of the list of tables will have "LIST OF TABLES (CONT.)" centered one inch from the top of the page. Observe the specific column headings ("Table" and "Page" in upper and lowercase letters) shown in Figure 3-5.

LIST OF ILLUSTRATIONS

Figure	Title	Page
2-1	System Flowchart	2-2
3-1	ABC Input Form	3-2
3-2	DEF Input Form	3-4
5-1	Audit Report Example	5-6
5-2	Personnel Report Example	5-9

FIGURE 3-4. List of Illustrations Example

LIST OF TABLES

Table		Page
3-1	ABC Card Type	3-2
3-2	DEF Card Type	3-5
6-1	Error Messages	6-2

FIGURE 3-5. List of Tables Example

CHAPTERS

The information in a manual will be divided into individual chapters. According to a possible set of standards, each chapter will be identified on top of its first page numerically and by title in the center, one inch from the top. For example:

```
                    CHAPTER 4
                 OUTPUT REPORTS
```

Chapters can be divided into sections (if necessary). Each section also may be identified numerically and by title. The section identification must be placed by the left-hand margin. The numbering scheme used is discussed in Subsection 3.2.2. For example:

```
                 4.1 SAVINGS REPORT
```

In turn, sections can be subdivided into subsections (if necessary), identified numerically and by title. Again, the subsection identification must be placed by the left-hand margin. The numbering scheme used is discussed in Subsection 3.2.2. For example:

```
4.1.1 REGULAR SAVINGS—BY ACCOUNT NUMBER REPORT
```

APPENDICES

Appendices can be used to amplify the manual narrative with technical data. They should only contain such technical data as calculations, tables, formulas, etc. Error and system messages should never be placed in an appendix. They should be listed and explained in a separate chapter.

An appendix will be identified by a capital letter and title on top of its first page in the center, one inch from the top. For example:

```
                    APPENDIX A
                SYSTEM CALCULATIONS
```

GLOSSARY

The glossary should define those terms that might prove trouble-some for the user. The terms and their definitions must be placed alphabetically. As with the index, a glossary should have its own unique page numbering scheme, which is explained in Subsection 3.2.2. An effective format which can be used for a glossary is shown in Figure 3-6.

GLOSSARY

ALPHANUMERIC CHARACTER	— A character consisting of an alphabetic character (A-Z) or the numeric digits (0-9).
BIT	— Acronym for binary digit.
CPU	— Central processing unit of the computer; its arithmetic unit and registers. Sometimes it is called the mainframe.
DATA BASE	— A collection of logically-related files containing data and structural information.
FILE	— A collection of related records treated as a unit.

FIGURE 3-6. Glossary Example

INDEX

The index has a great impact on any manual. When used, it consists of an alphabetic listing with its own unique page numbering scheme, which is explained in Subsection 3.2.2. When typeset, two columns must be placed on a page. Each alphabetic group will be preceded by the appropriate capital letter (in a bold typeface) centered over the column. Cross-referencing of information should be done when necessary. Refer to Figure 3-7 for an example.

INDEX

A	C
Alpha processing module, 2-22	Calling program, 2-21, 2-30
ANOP, 6-3, 8-33 rules, 6-3 statement form, 6-3	Call statement, 5-1, 5-2, 5-5
Appendices, 1-2, A-1, B-1, C-1	**E**
Assembler interface for the ANSI COBOL external read modules, example of, 3-6	EBGRAPH precautions, 5-6 E card, 8-5, 8-16, 8-30
	F
B	F card, 3-16, 3-17, 3-18, 5-5
Binary signed numbers, 3-7	Fixed length records, 3-13
Bit definition, 3-7	Format type codes, table of, 5-42

FIGURE 3-7. Index Example

An index will be identified, for instance, by the word "INDEX" on top of its first page in the center in capital letters, one inch from the top. Succeeding pages of the index will have "INDEX (CONT.)" in the same position.

READERS COMMENTS PAGE

If a readers comments page is necessary, it should appear after the index as the last page. It must be of a heavier stock paper to satisfy mailing requirements and be perforated one inch from the manual spine to permit removal.

The front portion of the page should identify the manual and indicate that comments are welcome to improve manual usefulness and readability. In addition, the following pertinent questions should be listed concerning the contents:

- Does this publication meet your needs?
- Did you find the material easy to understand, complete, well-illustrated and written for your level?
- Did you effectively implement the (name of system) with information from this manual?
- Did you attend a training session?

In addition, the statement, "Please indicate any comments in the space provided, if you have any," should be included. This allows readers to express their views and needs. It provides a line of communication between the writer and reader, helping each to perform his or her job effectively.

On the lower portion of the page, instructions should be briefly shown regarding the form's disposition:

> FOLD THE FORM ON THE DOTTED LINES, STAPLE, AND MAIL. No postage is necessary if the form is mailed in the United States.

These instructions should be typeset according to standards, such as using an eight point bold typeface.

The back portion of the page should contain the company's mailing address and necessary post office information in the center of the page. Dotted lines will be situated above and below this mailing information, dividing the back page into thirds to allow folding.

NOTE: Contact your local post office for exact requirements concerning the graphics necessary for business reply mail. For your information, a typical example using the aforementioned standards is shown in Figure 3-8.

READERS
  COMMENTS

We welcome comments on the usefulness and
readability of this manual. Your comment will
help us improve the quality of future publications.

THE DATA ANALYZER
TECHNICAL REFERENCE MANUAL

	YES	NO
● Does this publication meet your needs?	☐	☐
● Did you find the material:		
— Easy to read and understand?	☐	☐
— Complete?	☐	☐
— Well illustrated?	☐	☐
— Written for your level?	☐	☐
● Did you effectively implement The Data Analyzer with information from this manual?	☐	☐
● Did you attend a training session?	☐	☐

● Please indicate any comments in the space provided,
if you have any.

FOLD THE FORM ON THE DOTTED LINES, STAPLE, AND MAIL.
No postage is necessary if the form is mailed in the United States.

FIGURE 3-8. Readers Comments Page Example
(Reprinted with permission of TSI International, Ltd.)

fold

fold

||||

NO POSTAGE
NECESSARY
IF MAILED
IN THE
UNITED STATES

BUSINESS REPLY MAIL

FIRST CLASS   PERMIT NO. 66   MONTVALE, N.J.

Postage will be paid by addressee

**PROGRAM
PRODUCTS**

Program Products Incorporated
95 Chestnut Ridge Road
Montvale, New Jersey 07645

ATTENTION: Documentation Department

fold

fold

PROGRAM PRODUCTS INCORPORATED

Corporate Headquarters
95 Chestnut Ridge Road
Montvale, New Jersey 07645
201 / 391-9800

Western Office
14661 Myford Road - Suite B
Tustin, California 92680
714/730-1737

Midwest Office
2115 Butterfield Road - Suite 200
Oakbrook, Illinois 60521
312/932-6745

Southern Office
6520 Powers Ferry Road
Atlanta, Georgia 30339
404/955-5659

Southwest Office
One North Park East - Suite 200
Dallas, Texas 75231
214/369-6477

FIGURE 3-8. (continued)

3.2.2 Numbering Scheme

To operate effectively, a manual must have a flexible numbering scheme which covers three basic areas: chapters, sections, subsections and appendices; figures and tables; and pages. This modular approach is designed to assist the writer in developing a manual and the reader in accessing data more easily.

CHAPTERS, SECTIONS, SUBSECTIONS AND APPENDICES

Example standards for each of these areas are:

- Each chapter will be identified with an arabic numeral; for example: CHAPTER 1, CHAPTER 2, etc.
- Each section number will reflect the chapter it is in and its sequence in the chapter; for example, in Chapter 1 the sections are numbered 1.1, 1.2, 1.3, etc.
- Each subsection number will reflect the chapter it is in, its sequence in the chapter, and its numerical sequence in the section; for example, in Chapter 1 the subsections are numbered 1.1.1, 1.1.2, 1.1.3, etc.
- Each appendix will be identified with a letter; for example: APPENDIX A, APPENDIX B, etc.

FIGURES AND TABLES

Example standards for each of these areas are:

- Each figure number will reflect the chapter it is in and its sequence in the chapter; for example, in Chapter 1 the figures are numbered 1-1, 1-2, 1-3, etc.
- Each table number will reflect the chapter it is in and its sequence in the chapter; for example, in Chapter 1 the tables are numbered 1-1, 1-2, 1-3, etc.

NOTE: When reference is made to a figure or table in the manual text, ensure that the figure or table follows the reference as closely as possible.

PAGES

Example standards for page numbering are:

- The front matter will be unique in the pagination process. These pages will be numbered in the low left- or right-hand side using small roman numerals; for example: i, ii, iii, iv, v, vi, etc.
- The page numbers of the chapter will reflect the chapter they are in and their sequence in the chapter. They will be numbered in the lower left- or right-hand side; for example, the pages in Chapter 1 will be 1-1, 1-2, 1-3, etc.
- The page numbers of the appendices will reflect the appendix they are in and their sequence in the appendix. They will be numbered in the lower left- or right-hand side; for example, the pages in Appendix A will be A-1, A-2, A-3, etc.; the pages in Appendix B will be B-1, B-2, B-3, etc.

NOTE: If there are many appendices, ensure that the letter designations, G and I, are not used. They are the page designations for the glossary and index, respectively.

- The page numbers of the glossary will show they are part of the glossary and their sequence. They will be numbered in the lower left- or right-hand side; for example: G-1, G-2, G-3, etc.
- The page numbers of the index will show they are part of the index and their sequence. They will be numbered in the lower left- or right-hand side; for example: I-1, I-2, I-3, etc.

Refer to Subsection 3.2.3 for information concerning the conditions under which all page numbers will appear.

3.2.3 Manual Layout

If pages are to be printed on one side, page numbers will be placed, according to example standards, on the lower right-hand side, one-half inch from the bottom and one inch from the right outer edge.

If pages are to be printed on both sides, the front matter, chapters, appendices, glossary and index will start on a right-hand page.

Right-hand pages will be odd-numbered. The page number will appear, by example standards, one-half inch from the bottom and one inch from the right outer edge.

Left-hand pages will be even-numbered. The page number will appear one-half inch from the bottom and one inch from the left outer edge.

Each printed page will have standardized margins; for example:

- Left- and right-hand side margins—one inch.
- Upper margin—one inch.
- Lower margin—one inch (as closely as possible).

NOTE: More precise requirements dealing with spacing between sections, subsections, figures, and tables are discussed in Table 8-1 because of their impact on the appearance of a manual.

3.2.4 Figure and Table Titles

Figures and tables within the body of the manual text must be identified by title in addition to their sequential number in the chapter. As such, they must adhere to certain standards to maintain consistency, which are outlined under their relative categories.

FIGURE TITLES

The title of a figure must consist, for instance, of upper and lower case letters, and be centered under the figure with its identifying number. For example:

Figure 2-1. System Flow Chart

If the figure consists of two or more pages, the same title would be placed on each page in the same position. In addition, the number of pages and the page position in the series would follow in parentheses. This technique allows the writer to keep track of all pieces of artwork, and lets the reader know how many parts constitute an illustration. For example, if a figure consists of six pages, the following figure title would appear under the figure on the first page:

```
Figure 2-1. System Flow Chart (Page 1 of 6)
```

The numbering scheme process would continue until the sixth page. The following figure title would then appear under the figure on that page:

```
Figure 2-1. System Flow Chart ( Page 6 of 6)
```

TABLE TITLES

According to example standards, the title of a table must consist of capital letters and be centered over the table with its identifying number. For example:

```
TABLE 6-1. ERROR MESSAGES
```

If the table consists of two or more pages, the same title would be placed on each of these pages with the abbreviation, CONT., placed after the title. For example:

```
TABLE 6-1. ERROR MESSAGES (CONT.)
```

3.2.5 Artwork Reductions and Type Size

Those areas of artwork addressed by the detailed manual standards consist of two areas: reductions and type sizes.

REDUCTIONS

All artwork should fit within the limits of the established margins. When it is too large, the artwork should be reduced to fit in the assigned space. Assistance in determining the correct percentage to reduce the artwork can be obtained from the art department or freelance artist, as the case may be.

TYPE SIZE

Depending on the typeface used in the manual, standards such as the following type sizes should be observed.

- The basic text of the manual, body of the front matter, and index body will be in ten point medium.
- Headings of the front matter, chapters, appendices, glossary and index will be in eleven point bold.
- The section and subsection headings will be in ten point bold.
- Figure titles will be in ten point italic under the illustrations.
- Table headings and column headings in the table will be in ten point bold.
- Any emphasized text will be in ten point bold.
- The word "NOTE" in all notes found in the text will be in ten point bold.
- The title on the title page will be in eleven point bold.
- The version number on the version number and copyright page will be in eleven point bold; the copyright information will be in eight point meduim.

NOTE: The method of measuring type sizes is the point system. It is based on the pica which is equivalent to 12 point and equal to 4.233 mm.

3.2.6 Updating of Manuals

The following rules must be observed in updating manuals:

- If information is changed on a page or new information is added, that area on the page will be identified with a black vertical line in the outer margin opposite the change.
- If new pages of information fall at the end of a portion of manual text, they will be numbered following the normal numbering sequence. For example, if the last page of a series is 2-10 and two new pages are added, they would be numbered 2-11 and 2-12.
- If new pages must be inserted between existing pages, their numbering sequence will deviate from the standard. The

new pages will carry the number of the existing page that immediately precedes them, yet they will be numbered such that they will not be greater than the following existing page. This is done by placing a small letter adjacent to the page number, in alphabetic sequence; for example, if three pages of text are to be inserted between pages 4-13 and 4-14, they would be numbered 4-13a, 4-13b, and 4-13c. At some point, many pages may be numbered in this manner. When this occurs, they should be renumbered sequentially and the appropriate changes made to the table of contents and index. For further information concerning the conditions under which this page numbering standard occurs in manual maintenance, refer to Section 7.2.

- A revision number and date will appear on the lower portion of each "changed" or "new" page opposite the page number as follows.

CHANGE 3 - 2 FEBRUARY 82

With the issue of each set of changes, a "List of Effective Pages" must be sent to ensure that the publication is up-to-date. It has a two-fold purpose: to help the writer maintain a current inventory of manual pages, and to keep the reader aware of any changes that might affect the data in the manual. Refer to Chapter 7 for further information concerning the List of Effective Pages and the proper maintenance of manuals.

3.2.7 Use of Notes

Notes used throughout the manual text must be consistent in format. For example:

NOTE: Ensure the following procedure is used under the conditions described in Chapter 3.

"NOTE," by example standards, is always in a bold typeface to ensure that it is noticed by the reader.

CHAPTER FOUR

Accessing Data Sources

The application of a basic documentation policy and standards is essential in the development of any manual; however, to be successful, sufficient technical data must be available with which to work. With this in mind, the writer must access as many data sources as possible. Those which provide the most meaningful information for the writer's purposes are:

- The requirements analysis, basic project plan, functional specifications and system specifications.
- Additional written or printed technical material (e.g., code listings, notes and memos, and minutes of meetings.)
- Interviews with those members of the technical staff responsible for a system's development.

Each of these data sources is discussed in Sections 4.1 through 4.3.

In addition, a unique data source exists that the writer can access with some effort. That is working with the actual software package and associated equipment until he or she acquires a sufficient amount of practical knowledge. The hands-on experience gained will be particularly useful in the preparation of user and installation manuals. A discussion of this aspect of data gathering is found in Section 4.4.

Once the necessary information has been obtained, the writer must determine the extent of the available information needed to address effectively the reader audience. This is necessary in developing a manual to fit within the bounds of the original outline, while providing sufficient intelligible data for the reader. The proper manner in which this function is performed is discussed in Section 4.5.

4.1   STUDYING FORMAL SOURCE DOCUMENTS

Initially any project involving the development of a computer system and its internal programs requires the preparation of certain documents by management and the technical staff. They are designed to assist the programmer and data processing personnel in creating their particular portion of the computer system and keeping management appraised of the system's growth and cost.

These documents (in order of preparation) include a requirements analysis, basic project plan, functional specifications, and system specifications. Once written, they become important sources of data that the writer should access in the development of his manual.

They play an important role in the evolution of a design plan over a period of time. However, these technical documents are not static; they constantly change with the introduction of new ideas and objectives. In turn, the development of any manuals which depend on these technical documents for information is greatly affected.

The structure of these documents must be understood by the writer before interpreting any technical information. To provide some idea of the contents of each one, a brief summary of their contents and functions in manual development is provided in Subsections 4.1.1 through 4.1.4.

NOTE: The technical documents that are described may differ slightly from similar documents in other data processing facilities. This is due to a difference in each facility's requirements. In addition, the variations in hardware configuration associated with different software packages may demand additional data.

4.1.1 Requirements Analysis

When the idea for a particular system is born, specific requirements must be defined by management. From this definition, a technical staff member or outside consultant, as the case may be, can initiate an in-depth study. The resulting requirements analysis will clearly and accurately define the objectives and goals of management in developing the prospective system.

By studying this formalized document, the writer can gain an insight into management's initial thoughts concerning the system. To determine whether this was done, the writer should ask the following questions:

- What was the purpose in developing the system?
- What was needed to ensure the swift development of the system?

If the answers are satisfactory, the writer will have a firm base from which to develop his understanding of the system. The next technical document that he or she must access is the basic project plan, which naturally evolves from the requirements analysis.

4.1.2 The Basic Project Plan

The next step in the development of a system is the basic project plan. Its purpose is to indicate how the objectives and goals of management will be accomplished in developing a particular computer system. Within the framework of this document, the following basic areas of information are covered:

- *System definition.* This section of the plan defines the system in general terms, identifying its most important features. Supplementing the text is information to identify those enhancements that can be added now and at a future date. In addition, the system's shortcomings are described fully and why they cannot be eliminated at the present time.
- *Software requirements.* Certain areas of information concerning assembly, compilation, and linkage are described (e.g., languages used and necessary utilities). In addition, the following information should be included:

  - The minimum amount of memory required for execution.
  - The maximum amount of memory that can be used.
  - Software necessary for the support of the system (runtime libraries and utilities, languages, etc.).
  - Execution time for specific types of associated hardware.

- The precision with which calculations are made during processing.

- *I/O resources.* Input and output resources are identified. In addition, conditions under which they are used are described fully (i.e., the kind of data used as input and output for each resource, control functions, and available error facilities).

- *Data base structure.* A data base is a collection of logically-related files that contains data and structural information. A clear definition of these areas is essential in planning a system, as a data base is one of its most important features. Because of its impact on system design, it must be well thought out. Therefore, the manner and method for accessing the data base must be described.

- *Performance considerations.* This area of information contains:

  - Specific conditions that might affect the internal or external performance or reliability of the system.
  - Actions that can eliminate adverse incidents.
  - Options available to improve the performance of a system.

- *Overall system plan.* Within this section, the following areas of information are described:

  - The documentation required to design the system, and code and debug its programs.
  - The extent of the system's functional specifications (i.e., when it will be ready for distribution to the staff, and what areas it will address).
  - The length of time necessary to design the system.

Once it has been determined how long it will take to design the system, all phases in its development must be identified. For each phase, the following questions must be answered:

- What will be accomplished in the development phase?
- How long will it take to code and debug the programs in the system? (It should be noted that coding is contingent on data and machine availability. These factors can have a severe impact on the design schedule and budget.)

- What types of documentation will be developed and to whom will they be addressed?
- How long will it take to develop all documentation for the system?
- What resources are required to support the system and update the documentation as the software is enhanced?

Finally an overall schedule must be included to show the life cycle of the system, starting from its initial conception to its implementation. All phases within this schedule must be shown with their estimated beginning and completion dates.

By studying carefully the six areas within a basic project plan, the approach that was taken to develop the system will become apparrent. The information that forms the basic technical document allows the writer to see the system from management's viewpoint. It is designed to particularly emphasize the time schedules necessary to complete the system, cost considerations, and the system's ultimate use. In its entirety, the basic project plan is an excellent reference source which the writer should use as an introduction to the system.

4.1.3 Functional Specifications

The purpose of the functional specifications is to define the system fully, describe its processing cycle, and identify those conditions under which it will operate.

Within the framework of the functional specifications, the following areas of information are covered:

- *System definition.* This section expands on the areas of information outlined in the basic project plan. The system is described in more specific terms (e.g., more detailed information on features and future enhancements, and system limitations). In addition, it is noted whether the proposed system will affect other software products currently produced by the company.
- *System installation.* The following information is provided in this section:
  - Software and hardware needed to install the system.
  - Files that will be released and their form.

— Physical requirements (e.g., 110V or 220V power source).
— Related environmental conditions (e.g., required humidity and temperature).

In addition, maintenance considerations are addressed. It is shown how changes are to be released, and what software and hardware requirements are needed for an update.

- *Environment.* The operating conditions under which the proposed system will be used are described in this section. The hardware and software necessary to support the system effectively are shown. The basic types of software that should be listed include utilities, operating systems, and languages. In addition to hardware and software considerations, the users of the system are identified and the limits of their expertise indicated.

- *Detailed system description.* This section of the functional specifications describes what the system does and identifies its major components (i.e., programs or blocks of programs). To provide a better idea of the system's capabilities, examples showing how the system is used are shown. In addition, how the system would fare in the competitive marketplace with other products is discussed.

- *File structures.* A file is a collection of related records treated as a unit. Clear definition of these structures is essential in planning a system, particularly the identification of individual file structures that provide access to the system (e.g., input, output and work files.)

- *On-line user command data.* If the system is on-line, the various user commands and their associated terminal screen displays and messages are shown.

- *Error conditions.* This section completely describes those error conditions under which input and output resources could be used, as well as the facilities available for error recovery.

- *Glossary.* The last section of the functional specifications identifies those terms peculiar to the specific system being developed. All terms should be in alphabetic order and defined fully.

Functional specifications can educate the writer by isolating and describing key areas of a system. Further information concerning the internal structure of a system and the fundamentals necessary to ensure design consistency is provided in the system specifications.

4.1.4 System Specifications

The purposes of the system specifications are:

- To provide direction for those programmers working on the system, ensuring that their thoughts are organized in the same manner.
- To describe the system so that each programmer can understand and document his or her phase of it.

This document can be expanded during the development of a system to suit its designers. Eventually it will be used for maintenance, once the system has been finalized.

Within the framework of the system specifications, the following areas of information are covered:

- *System identification.* This information identifies the system and all associated references. It includes:
  - System name.
  - Project number.
  - Reference to the functional specifications.
  - Other references and supporting documents.

- *Design philosophy.* This section provides an overview of the system, highlighting any unique features. It must be assumed that the programmer reading this area of the document understands the functional specifications and is familiar with common programming techniques. Supplementing the overview is a verbal or pictorial description of the general flow of data and the controls governing that flow.

  In addition, the following information must be present for the design philosophy to be pertinent:
  - The basis for structuring and organizing the system as it is.
  - Other design alternatives that were studied and, eventually, rejected.

- *Data structure.* If the data structures are fully described elsewhere, reference should be made to the appropriate listing or document. Any additional information discussing the order or organization of the data must appear in this section of the system specifications, including:

  − Files.
  − Record formats.
  − Lists.
  − Arrays.
  − Tables.

- *System structure.* Information is presented in such a way as to show how the system works, highlighting special design details. The structure can be described effectively through liberal use of illustrations, such as:

  − Tree and hierarchy diagrams.
  − Interface points.
  − Control transfer points.
  − Standard routines.
  − Logic control tables.

- *Physical organization of the system.* To provide an accurate picture of how the system is organized, certain areas of information are described, including:

  − Memory maps.
  − Overlay structure.
  − Relocatable modules.
  − Generated segments.
  − Link edit considerations.
  − Block diagrams.

- *Conventions used in system design.* During the design phase of the system, specific conventions must be employed to maintain consistency and order. To achieve this condition, the following areas of information are covered:

  − Interface considerations.
  − File formats.

- Data formats.
- Any global variables.
- Labels and naming conventions.
- Subroutine linkage.
- Table processing.
- Register usage.
- Interrupt processing.
- Stack usage.
- Documentation conventions (as defined by the documentation standards).

In addition, all conventions that must be violated in the design of a system are identified, with the results of the violations.

- *Modules.* All major modules are identified, and a brief description of their purpose given. In addition, the following information is shown for each module:

  - Register and global values.
  - Parameter input.
  - Linkage in.
  - Called modules.
  - Error checking.
  - Error conditions.
  - Error exits.
  - Register state, stack state, and data value on error exit.
  - Parameter output.
  - Normal exit.
  - Register, stack and data values at exit.
  - Module size.
  - External/internal references.

- *Errors.* This section of the system specification outlines any special handling of errors (e.g., cause, error message, operator action and result, system action and result, and the effect on the system).

- *Messages.* Each message generated by the system must be identified. Also, the following related information is shown:

  - Purpose of message.
  - Meaning.

          – Operator action.
          – System action.

- *System testing procedures.* This area of information is essential to validate a program's integrity. Within this test framework, internal diagnostics and test procedures exist that must be identified. In addition, any software used for testing purposes must be shown.

NOTE: This phase of a system design is often neglected. Its importance should not be underestimated.

- *Software aids.* Often, during the design of a system, certain utility programs may be needed. If so, these aids (e.g., software tools for development and testing, and debugging aids) are listed in this section.
- *Security considerations.* To prevent the compromise of data in a proposed system, specific security measures must be taken. For this reason, this section of the system specifications should describe the security aspects of the system fully.

NOTE: In most cases, the information in this section may not be available for use in a manual. However, if the manual is being written for the managerial level and above, this may not be the case.

- *Future development.* This section of the system specifications is reserved for the listing of proposed enhancements and any information related to them.

System specifications are instrumental in finalizing the design of a system. Therefore, the information that is extracted from this document should be utilized by the writer in developing a manual. This is particularly true toward the end of a system's design when the information is near finalization.

4.2   EXAMINING ADDITIONAL WRITTEN OR PRINTED TECHNICAL MATERIAL

After reading and understanding the requirements analysis, basic project plan, functional specifications and system specifications, the writer should investigate other areas of information. The voluminous amount of technical material generated during a system's development represents a fertile area to research. The types of information that may be available include:

- *Code listings.* These printed documents are generated as a system is being designed. Their basic content should conform to those technical documents described in Section 4.1. They act as an excellent reference source for the writer, clarifying vague areas. In addition, they are a good check point, particularly if a programmer has deviated from the established norm in system development (i.e., not following the established functional or system specifications in designing his or her particular area of the system).

During the development of a system, the following types of information might be found in a typical code listing:

- Subroutine definitions.
- Entry and exit points for the subroutines.
- Method in which arguments are passed to the subroutines.
- Conventions being followed in system development.
- System limitations.
- Constraints followed by the subroutines.
- Error handling procedures.

- *Notes and memos.* An invaluable source of information can be found in notes and memos that passed between management and the system designers before and during the development phase. By defining who the key individuals of a project were and gaining access to any notes and memos, the writer can trace the entire life of a system from its inception to its implementation. The system can be seen from the designer's viewpoint. Therefore, regard any notes and memos as an integral part of data gathering, one that illuminates the human side of a system's development.
- *Minutes of meetings.* Normally many meetings occur periodically while a system is being designed. Their purpose usually is to discuss design changes, problems that may occur, conflicts to the existing schedules, or other items affecting the

evolution of a system. When these meetings occur, minutes are usually kept and passed out to the participants. Like notes and memos, minutes of meetings are an invaluable source of system data. All of this information is only available to the writer who has the perseverance and desire to obtain complete and technically accurate data.

It would be to your benefit to attend any meetings held throughout the development of a system, if that is possible. Although detailed minutes cover the more salient points of a meeting, the writer's actual participation would produce an appreciation for those problems faced by the staff designers.

Up to this point, you should have accumulated the necessary technical documents (described in Section 4.1) and other written and printed material generated by management and the staff designers. The bulk of this data should give you a good starting point from which to conduct interviews of key staff members. This is necessary before data can be reviewed and organized.

4.3 INTERVIEWING MEMBERS OF THE TECHNICAL STAFF

To expand the data that has already been gathered, the writer must interview those members of the technical staff responsible for a system's development. An effective interview allows you to answer nagging questions and clear up vague areas. It is a unique opportunity for the writer to pick the staff's brains to obtain a more complete picture of a system.

The successful completion of an interview can be achieved only by adhering to certain guidelines:

- *Know the people involved.* Personalities are an integral part of any interview. If you maintain a basic rapport with these people, the interviews will be successful. Therefore, ensure that you understand their idiosyncracies and basic personality traits. They play a big role in your being able to extract the information you desire.

- *Generally understand the data that require clarification.* For an interview to run smoothly, you must know your subject to some degree. If you do not, the basic rapport that was initially established will be strained.
- *Establish a list of questions.* If your questions are vague, you will waste your time and that of the staff member. They must be complete, and designed so as not to cause any embarrassment for either party.
- *Do not write every word.* When writing notes at an interview, use your own version of shorthand. Nothing is more distracting to a person being interviewed than having to repeat what was said or talking slowly for the benefit of the interviewer.
- *Use a tape recorder in the interview.* It is an invaluable tool that captures the entire conversation. It is difficult to write notes and keep track of everything said at an interview; a tape recorder provides a solution to this problem. In addition, time will be saved.
- *Recap your data.* Once an interview is completed, rewrite your written notes and transcribe all important points from the taped interview. Then organize the information into some semblance of order. When it has been deciphered and organized, it can be added to the data you have already gathered.

The successful interview is one in which the writer and staff member each gain something. The writer receives all the data that he or she desires, and an understanding of the problems that are faced in the design of a system. On the other hand, the staff member has a better feel for the writer's problems and needs. In addition, by talking about the system, the staff member might find some inconsistencies in the system design that could subsequently be corrected.

4.4 GAINING HANDS-ON EXPERIENCE WITH THE SYSTEM

Often, it benefits the writer actually to manipulate data and participate in the daily operation of the system about which he or she is writing.

This is particularly true in the case of user and installation manuals, which require verification of the steps necessary to implement a particular system function.

As with any function, repetition of individual steps in its performance creates a better understanding of it and its relationship to the system. Continual use of the system's features gives the writer more confidence using the system and understanding its more elusive points.

This manipulation of data is particularly essential if the system has been developed with on-line capabilities. In this sense, it allows you to:

- View the screen formats of messages as they appear on the screen once you enter data via the terminal keyboard.
- Generate actual data on the screen that can be copied and used as examples in your manual. Refer to Figure 5–6 for an illustration of how the use of a screen format can be effective and how it is used in a step-by-step procedure.

In whatever manner data is applied to a system, ensure that you completely understand how it is entered, processed and, eventually, stored or generated. This is only possible if you actually work with the software.

4.5   DETERMINING THE EXTENT OF A MANUAL'S COVERAGE

Once all the data has been assembled, and before it can be applied to the organized structure of a manual, the writer must determine the most effective amount of data necessary to describe a system for the user audience. This is necessary to develop a manual that is meaningful and written in the most simple and nonrepetitive manner.

To achieve this goal, the writer must study all the assembled data, adhering to the following guidelines:

- *Know the user audience* (i.e., their needs, expertise, terminology with which they are familiar, and their weaknesses). With this knowledge, the writer can sift through the different types of data and intelligently determine the proper amount of data for the user audience. Originally, in developing its documentation policy, management should have determined those audiences using company manuals. The writer should then refine this audience definition to apply to his or her particular needs.

- *Be thoroughly familiar with the technical material.* Determining whether various areas of data should be used hinges on the writer's knowledge of the system and its applicability to appropriate areas of the manual. The application of the selected material to the needs of the user audience must be done carefully so as not to eliminate pertinent data.
- *Use a detailed and well-structured outline of the manual.* Once the data has been studied in the light of the user's needs, apply it to the existing outline. In this manner, the writer can see how the selected data would fit most effectively into the proposed manual's structure. In addition, the amount of data necessary to describe each area within the manual can be determined.

If you follow these guidelines, a picture will evolve of the most effective amount of data to describe a system for a particular user audience. Once this has been established, the pertinent data can be written and edited to fit into the organized structure of the prospective manual.

CHAPTER FIVE

Manual Preparation

Software manuals can be divided into four basic types: technical, user, installation and procedure. Each has a distinct purpose and is directed toward a specific audience. You, as the writer, must understand their individual traits before they can be prepared.

The *technical manual* is probably the most straightforward of all manuals. It has been a resident of the data processing community the longest; yet even though data processing has been in existence for some time, technical manuals for software are relative newcomers. Offshoots of the electronics industry, they developed with the tremendous growth of software into different forms that were barely readable.

Then and now, technical manuals come in every size and shape. Some are inadequate; others are poor. Therefore, one should raise the question, "Why has no one done anything about it?" An answer is that data processing managers thought documentation was something nice to have but that it could be done at a later time. The end result was an unorganized, poorly written, technically inaccurate piece of work. One purpose of this book is to change this point of view and present ways to produce good manuals.

The *user manual* grew out of the needs of the data processing community. Something more than a technical manual was needed. Users required a manual geared for their own environment, that could provide enough information written in just the right manner to do the job. The technical manual had all the information, but it had to be extracted and written to suit the user audiences.

Just how did the user manual originate? It likely cannot be determined; however, as the software industry grew, a need for diversified and complete documentation developed. When user manuals were written, they seemed to be mutant versions of technical manuals.

The same question arose as with technical manuals, "Why has no one done anything about it?" People tried, one supposes; but with other priorities and a lack of resources, unorganized and poorly written user manuals were produced.

To prepare an effective user manual, you must gear the manual for the specific user audience. The contents of the manual must be shaped into an instructional publication requiring a different organizational structure. Yet, its content must contain enough technical data of a general nature to act as a competent reference source. Further detailed information could be obtained from the technical manual, if desired.

The *installation manual* is an essential part of the software industry, required by technicians in the field to perform their jobs effectively. It provides a valuable service by containing information necessary to install and maintain a computer system. For this reason, it must be technically accurate and straightforward.

This type of manual must, of course, be based on an outline and adhere to a set of standards. As with any other type of writing, it must have a life cycle with specific time constraints.

Whatever course is taken with installation material, one thing is certain—it must be prepared with the technician in mind. All questions that he or she may have must be anticipated and answered in a format that is easy to read and reference.

The *procedure manual* is unusual in the data processing environment. It represents a vital link between the computer and the person who applies it to the daily work. Its functional application makes it a valuable document, particularly in a financial institution or large company. This type of manual even can be applied to smaller companies with a great deal of success.

This manual developed through a desire for organization and efficiency. With the growth of data processing, more and more functional problems grew which demanded immediate attention if companies were to exist.

To address these problems, procedure manuals had to deviate from the standards developed for technical, user and installation manuals. When written, individual procedures require a totally different point of view than that expressed in other manuals. Individual procedures must be geared for specific users. These users require written data that must be simple and adhere to a set structure consistent for each procedure.

In one respect, however, the procedure manual is similar to a user manual—it is instructional in nature. Its purpose is to explain a particular function or group of related functions to a specific person or group of persons. Because of its very nature, the procedure manual constantly changes. New procedures are being created; old ones are being deleted. In a sense, it is not so formal as a technical, user or installation manual. Yet, with constant use it has a sizeable impact on the efficiency of the daily work flow in the data processing facility.

To describe manual preparation effectively, Chapter 5 is organized in the following manner: Functions common to the technical, user, and installation manuals are outlined in Section 5.1; functions common to each type of manual are discussed in Sections 5.2 through 5.4. However, because of its unusual characteristics, the procedure manual is described in Section 5.5. Each section is geared toward helping the writer to understand the basic procedures of manual development. Further, certain techniques have been included that should provide additional insight into the formulation and preparation of written material.

5.1 TECHNICAL, USER, AND INSTALLATION MANUALS

Preparing each type of manual requires twelve specific functions:

- Determining the writing priority.
- Writing material that flows.
- Using notes to emphasize.
- Numbering sections and subsections.
- Identifying data within sections and subsections.
- Referencing in the text.
- Using tables.
- Using illustrations.
- Using key letters to explain data and coding.
- Formulating appendices.

- Preparing front tables.
- Preparing an index.

5.1.1   Determining the Writing Priority

At this point, the manual outline is complete, the data organized in convenient folders, and the preliminary artwork sent to the art department. Your next concern is how to begin the actual writing. The following order of writing priority should ease you into the manual gradually and allow you to get acquainted with the technical material further.

THE INTRODUCTORY CHAPTER

This chapter introduces the reader to the manual, describing its purpose in simple terms. In addition, it describes each chapter and appendix, giving the reader a general idea of how it is organized. This section of the chapter is, basically, an amplification of the manual outline. In addition, any unique standards and conventions should be included in this chapter to enlighten the reader. Through the basic structure of the manual and how it is organized, you establish a firm base for the reader to start technical inquiries into the computer system.

By starting with this chapter, you are introducing the manual to the reader and acquainting him or her with its contents, as well as introducing the manual to yourself. You are taking that initial plunge that will provide familiarity with the construction of the manual. Remember, easing into the actual task of writing will allow you eventually to become confident in your ability. As you proceed, this confidence will grow and you will be able to cope with problems more readily.

SYSTEM OVERVIEW CHAPTER

Preparation of a system overview brings you to an important point in your writing. When it is complete, you should have a good idea of how the system works, its purpose, and how it interrelates with other systems. This chapter must be written in a general manner, because it is designed simply to acquaint the reader with the system rather than provide all the specific details. More detail, of course, will be necessary in technical and installation manuals.

CHAPTERS OF INCREASING COMPLEXITY

The balance of the chapters in your manual must be judged according to their complexity. My recommendation is to start with the simplest one first. By the time you reach the more detailed chapters, you will have developed a reasonable writing expertise. In addition, you should have a good idea of how the system works. As a general rule, the more you know about something, the better you can write about it.

APPENDICES

The appendices can be done at any time; however, leave them until the bulk of your manual is complete. They depart from the writing discipline because their function is to present technical formulas, technical calculations, listings, etc. Often, you will face a great deal of data that is difficult to present in narrative form in the main body of the manual. Therefore, the solution is to place this material in well-organized and detailed appendices.

GLOSSARY

As with the appendices, a glossary can be done at any time. Its purpose is to give the reader an understanding of the unique terminology in the manual. As such, it must be complete and structured in such a manner as to permit ease of referral.

TABLE OF CONTENTS, LIST OF ILLUSTRATIONS, AND LIST OF TABLES

At this point in the life cycle of a manual, all pages should be numbered. When this occurs, the front tables can be prepared. All sections and subsections must be identified in the table of contents, with their associated page numbers.

INDEX

The index represents the last step in writing a manual. While the front tables direct the reader to general blocks of information, an index is, by its nature, more specific. A complete index provides the reader with the ability to refer to a specific topic quickly and, ultimately, answer his or her questions. Instructions to prepare an index are shown in Subsection 5.1.12.

MISCELLANEOUS PAGES

Miscellaneous pages include the title page, copyright and version number page, and readers comments page. If you find time while writing the manual, prepare them. If not, leave them for last.

5.1.2 Writing Material That Flows

This aspect of writing is essential in all types of manuals. In technical manuals particularly, it is necessary to carry the reader from beginning to end, covering all aspects of a system or related technical subject. To do this, a writer must learn some basic techniques.

When preparing an outline, the blocks of information are defined. They should follow a certain sequence. Within each block of information, subdivisions should be established providing more specific details. Together, they demonstrate a system or subject flow. Using this detailed outline as the skeleton of your manual, fill in the pertinent information in such a manner as to carry the reader along between sentences, paragraphs, subsections, sections and chapters.

Certain techniques can be used to provide this continuity. They include: short, complete sentences and simple terminology, and key word and phrase use.

SHORT, COMPLETE SENTENCES AND SIMPLE TERMINOLOGY

To produce an easy moving piece of writing, use short complete sentences. This helps you in writing as well as the user in reading the material. These sentences can be tied together more easily than ones that are bulky and tedious. As a general rule, follow this policy in any technical, user or installation manual you write.

In line with this, use simple terminology and phrasing. Think of the person reading the manual. The simpler you write, the fewer problems will develop. The reader will not have to run to a dictionary everytime a complex word appears.

Simplicity in wordage and overall sentence structure is the key to a writer's success. Both these elements carry the reader along smoothly and provide the continuity of information that is so important.

KEY WORD AND PHRASE USE

This technique is used to carry the reader from sentence to sentence and paragraph to paragraph, as the case may be. A word or phrase is repeated in the beginning of a sentence or paragraph after appearing in the preceding sentence or paragraph. For example:

> After the Accepted Transactions File is sorted by the XXXXX program, the sorted data is processed by the *YYY program*. In the *YYY program*, the sorted data is placed on the ZZZZZ file.

Another method is to insert "also" or "in addition" when circumstances dictate their use. If you need to add further information about a certain topic, use one of these phrases. However, be careful not to overuse them.

5.1.3 Using Notes To Emphasize

Notes can be inserted sparingly throughout your manual text; however, they should be used only to provide emphasis to certain points. Their use can add a certain tone to the manual with no text restructuring.

When notes are written, ensure that they are short and meaningful. Notes should not run on for several paragraphs. Instead, they should be anywhere from one to four sentences. Beyond that, they lose their impact.

Notes can also be used to explain certain points in the preceding text. If some data requires explanation, place an asterisk after that word or phrase in the text. If another item on that page also requires explanation, place a double asterisk after that word or phrase in the text, etc. Then at the bottom of the page, place your explanatory notes using the following format:

> *NOTE:* *   Used as input to the XXXXXX System.
>   ** Is generated by the *YYYYYY* System.

Devise a format for your notes and use it throughout a manual. Do not fluctuate between one format and another. To see how notes could be presented, refer to the detailed documentation standards in Subsection 3.2.7.

5.1.4 Numbering Sections and Subsections

Apply the standards outlined in Subsection 3.2.2 in numbering the sections and subsections of the manual. They should follow the numbering scheme of your outline.

Sections and subsections have their own peculiar numbering scheme. For example, if a chapter was identified as Chapter 4 (Operating Instructions), the following would be the manner in which sections and subsections would be numbered:

4.1	DOS USER	(as the general category)
4.1.1	INITIAL PHASE	(the first operating phase in the series, etc.)

Never go beyond the subsection level (i.e., 4.1.1.1, using the previous example). It can be done, but the numbering scheme gets unwieldy and hard to control. It also detracts from the streamlined look you should try to build into your manual.

If additional levels of information beyond the subsection level are necessary, several devices can be used to extract you from this dilemma. Figure 5-1 illustrates several graphic techniques. Each level is highlighted and explanations included when necessary. Study the manner in which the various levels are shown and apply them to your own manuals.

Section
Level ──────▶ ## 4.7 ENTER STATEMENT

The ENTER statement is The Analyzer's optional procedural language statement. It is used to insert special processing instructions into a report request. The ENTER statement is expanded internally into DATATRAN® in the Extract Phase and FORTRAN in the Print Phase.

Capabilities of the ENTER statement include:

1. Performing arithmetic calculations.
2. Moving data from one field to another.
3. Performing comparisons to determine what instructions are to be executed next.
4. Branching from one logic point to another or repeating instructions that have already been executed.
5. Calling a subroutine.

Sections 4.7.1 - 4.7.2 explain the ENTER statement in detail and show its internal structure. Section 4.7.3 shows valid and invalid examples.

Subsection
Level ──────▶ ### 4.7.1 ENTER STATEMENT FORMAT

The ENTER statement is written as follows.

$$
\left[\underline{\text{ENTER, logic point,}} \left[\text{statement number} \right] \left\{ \begin{array}{l} \text{set statement} \\ \text{IF STATEMENT} \\ \text{GO TO STATEMENT} \\ \text{subroutine CALL STATEMENT} \\ \underline{\text{CONTINUE STATEMENT}} \end{array} \right\} \right]
$$

The ENTER keyword and comma following it identify the statement and are required.

**FIGURE 5-1. Techniques to Identify Levels
of Information Beyond the Subsection
(Reprinted with permission of TSI International Ltd.)**

A single ENTER statement may be continued to two or more cards. The continuation card starts with ENTER, (no logic point) followed by the remainder of the statement. The continuation must immediately follow the statement that it continues. If the continuation card is ENTER, XX, where XX is a valid logic point, the continuation is considered a new statement.

Subsection Level ⟶ ### 4.7.2 ENTER STATEMENT ELEMENTS

To utilize the ENTER statement effectively, it is necessary to understand its individual elements. Each element of the ENTER statement and related descriptive information follows.

First Level of Information Under the Subsection Level (The numbering scheme and highlighting of the major elements shows this first level.)

1. *logic point* is the logic point at which the instruction will be processed. (Refer to Chapter 2 for a system flow chart and explanation of logic points.)

The ENTER statement may be placed anywhere in the report request. The statements need not be in sequence by logic point (i.e., statements coded with a logic point of DT may physically precede those coded with a logic point of D1, even though D1 occurs prior to DT). They must be placed in the report request in the order in which they are to be executed within their respective logic points (i.e., if two statements are coded for logic point DT, they will be executed in the order in which they appear in the request).

NOTE: ENTER statement at Read Phase logic points (R0–R9) must appear in the first request.

FIGURE 5-1. (continued)

2. *statement number* identifies statement numbers used to skip from place to place within a phase of a request. Any statement may contain a statement number which must be five digits.

A maximum of 250 ENTER statements per phase of a report may have statement numbers (i.e., 250 in the Read Phase, 250 in the Extract Phase, and 250 in the Print Phase). No duplicate numbers are permitted within a phase. A recommended range of statement numbers is 50000–59999.

If an instruction refers to a statement number, the request must include another instruction with the number within the same phase. The Print Phase does contain standard-generated statement numbers, which may be referenced in ENTER instructions. These numbers must not be duplicated. (Refer to Appendix D for system-generated statement numbers.)

First Level of Information Under the Subsection Level (The numbering scheme and highlighting of the major elements shows this first level.)

3. *The procedure instruction* may be any of the following.
   a. The set of assignment statement.
   b. The IF STATEMENT.
   c. The GO TO or computed GO TO STATEMENT.
   d. The Subroutine CALL STATEMENT.
   e. The CONTINUE STATEMENT.

Formats and rules for use of these statements follow.

FIGURE 5-1. (continued)

Centering and Bold
Type Face Used to
Accentuate this First
Subdivision Under
the First Level of
Information, "The
procedure
instruction".

SET STATEMENT

The set statement is used to place data in a named data field.

Multiple set operations may be performed in the same ENTER statement by coding two or more set operations separated by a semicolon (;).

The set statement is written as follows.

$$\underline{\text{fieldname}} \quad [(\text{subscript})] \quad = \left\{ \begin{array}{l} \text{fieldname}\,[(\text{subscript})] \\ \text{literal} \\ \$ZERO \\ \$SPACE \\ \text{arithmetic expression} \end{array} \right\} \quad [;\ldots]$$

Each element of the set statement and descriptive information follows.

Note the
Breakdown of
Information
Under "Set
Statement".

1. *fieldname* is any field defined in the dictionary by a D, T, or G card, a NEWFLD statement, or an allowable reserve word (in Appendix B). A data fieldname in the file must not be used to the left of an equal sign in an ENTER statement at an A logic point. Fields changed in the Read Phase at logic points R0–R9 in the first request are changed for all reports in the run.

When a file field is changed at Read Phase logic points (R1-R8), that area of the input record is changed for all reports in the run. The value of any fields which redefine that portion of the input record are also changed.

When a file field is changed at a Print Phase logic point, the data is changed only for the named field. Each field occupies its own area on the extracted data record.

FIGURE 5-1. (continued)

Fields which redefined the same area in the input record do not redefine the same area in the extracted data record.

The field must be large enough to contain the data on the right of the equal sign. In an alphanumeric set statement (if the receiving field is larger than the data to be moved into it), the remaining positions will be padded with blanks. If the receiving field is smaller than the data to be moved into it, the data will be truncated to the length of the receiving field.

In numeric operations, the field must be large enough to hold all nonzero digits to the left of the real or implied decimal point. If the field is too small, the result is truncated on the left and no indication of truncation is given.

2. *subscript* may be an integer numeric literal or a numeric data name with integer values. A fieldname may be followed by a subscript if the field has been defined as an array (periodic or repeated field).

3. *= (equal sign)* is the required symbol of the set statement.

4. *fieldname (to the right of the equal sign)* is a field defined in the dictionary on a D, T, or G card, a NEWFLD, or an allowable reserve word (in Appendix B). It must be the same type (numeric or alphanumeric) as the field to the left of the equal sign. It may or may not be a subscripted field.

5. *literal* is a data value that is written directly into an ENTER instruction. It may be either numeric or alphanumeric.

Note the · Breakdown of Information Under "Set Statement".

FIGURE 5-1. (continued)

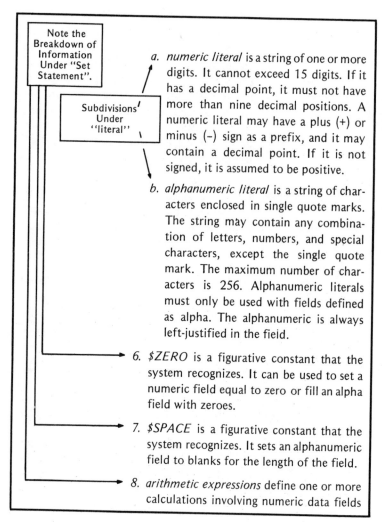

Note the Breakdown of Information Under "Set Statement".

Subdivisions Under "literal"

a. *numeric literal* is a string of one or more digits. It cannot exceed 15 digits. If it has a decimal point, it must not have more than nine decimal positions. A numeric literal may have a plus (+) or minus (–) sign as a prefix, and it may contain a decimal point. If it is not signed, it is assumed to be positive.

b. *alphanumeric literal* is a string of characters enclosed in single quote marks. The string may contain any combination of letters, numbers, and special characters, except the single quote mark. The maximum number of characters is 256. Alphanumeric literals must only be used with fields defined as alpha. The alphanumeric is always left-justified in the field.

6. *$ZERO* is a figurative constant that the system recognizes. It can be used to set a numeric field equal to zero or fill an alpha field with zeroes.

7. *$SPACE* is a figurative constant that the system recognizes. It sets an alphanumeric field to blanks for the length of the field.

8. *arithmetic expressions* define one or more calculations involving numeric data fields

FIGURE 5-1. (continued)

and/or numeric literals. The valid arithmetic symbols are as follows.

a. + for addition.
b. - for subtraction.
c. * for multiplication.
d. / for division.

Any number of parenthesized expressions are allowed to specify the order in which operations are to be computed. However, only one level of parentheses may be used (i.e., parentheses may not appear within parentheses except parentheses used for subscript notation).

Arithmetic expressions are evaluated from left to right. All multiplications and divisions are calculated before any additions and subtractions. Parenthesized expressions are resolved first. If an integer value is placed in a decimal field, the value to the right of the decimal point will be set to zero. If a decimal value is placed in an integer field, the decimal point and all decimal positions are truncated without rounding.

FIGURE 5-1. (continued)

As you can see, through manipulation of words and effective use of typography, the numbering problem has been addressed. In addition, the text is presented in a totally professional manner.

5.1.5 Identifying Data Within Sections and Subsections

Often information must be listed in a section or subsection. The simplest way to deal with this situation is to number each unit:

---

* The terminal screen formats that are used in the operation of the On-Line Analyzer under IMS are:

1. Master Screen
2. Request Creation
3. Request Submittal
4. Report Status
5. Report Display/Print

The numbers must be placed in line with the left-hand side of the paragraphs.

If information must be broken down under one or more of the numbered units, do it as follows:

---

* 4. *Blank lines.* The Analyzer automatically supplies blank lines at the following points:

    a. In the page title, if the request contains no TITLE statements and it specified the NOPGNO option.

    b. Between the page title and the first line of column headings.

    c. In place of column headings, if none of the data fields has a column heading.

    d. Between the column heading and the first detail line.

If, however, you want to emphasize certain points in the text of the manual and do not want to use a numbering scheme, use bullets:

---

* Prior to entering Analyzer statements on the Request Creation Screen, you should be aware of certain basic facts concerning this phase of processing:

● The ID entry field should be left blank except when copying pages from an existing request in your library. Refer to Section 4.2.2 to copy a library request.

No ID is needed for the current request even if you want to save it. In such a case, an ID is assigned when using the Request Submittal Screen to execute the request. Refer to Section 5.1.

● Preformatted keywords are for your convenience. They may be used or ignored but cannot be typed over.

● Statements function as described in the Data Analyzer Technical Reference Manual, except as noted.

● The END statement may be omitted on the last or only request.

---

*Reprinted with permission of TSI International Ltd.

Place the bullets in line with the left-hand side of the paragraphs. Use bullets for two or more items. *Never use a bullet for one item.*

5.1.6 Referencing in the Text

Referencing in any manual is critical. It is an effective tool that can assist the reader and writer to find a particular table, illustration, or section for specific details. However, this technique is only effective when used properly. To reference material, certain rules should be observed and maintained, if problems in manual development are to be avoided:

- Never reference a page number. When the pages change at some future date because of revision, your reference in the text will no longer be accurate.
- Always reference a section or subsection number, chapter number, table number or figure number, as the case may be. You have tighter control over this numbering scheme. Even if there are page changes in a revision, the reference numbers of these areas in the manual probably will not change. If they do, then adjust the reference in the text.
- If a numbering scheme is not used in your manual (*which I strongly advise against*), reference the title of the section or subsection, chapter, table or figure, as appropriate. It is not as effective and will cause the reader to search for a particular item. Remember, your primary concern is the reader. Therefore, make things as easy as possible for him or her.
- When initially referencing an illustration or table, the reference in the text should precede the item as closely as possible.
- Never say "see below," "see above," or any other such phrase in the manual text when referencing an item. A problem arises in the final typesetting or typing because the item may not be above, below, etc.
- When referencing an item, several phrases could be used, each of which is as good as the other. For example:

> Refer to Sections 5.1 through 5.5 for further information.

or

> See Sections 5.1 through 5.5 for further information.

5.1.7 Using Tables

Tables are a blessing for any writer. They are an effective tool that should be used when a great deal of technical data has to be documented, yet the complexity of this data makes it almost impossible to write in any sort of intelligible prose. This dilemma often can be circumvented by using a well-structured table.

A table will break the information down into concise units of information in a columnar form. This organized information can then be referenced easily from any point in the manual, something that is difficult to do if the information were absorbed in the text. This aspect of a table makes it highly desirable for the reader who needs to reference data quickly. Of course, you should establish a standard format when preparing tables. For example:

- The identifying number and title of the table must be centered over it.
- Columnar headings must be in a ten point bold typeface (in capital letters) and centered. Horizontal lines must separate the headings from the information.
- Vertical lines will divide each grouping of information, headed by the column heading.
- A single horizontal line will close the table.
- Notes should be placed at the end of the table usually, separated from the text by a horizontal line. Rules concerning notes should be observed. However, if certain points must be emphasized in the table, notes can be placed after the appropriate text.

Figure 5-2 illustrates these rules. Note that the aesthetic qualities of a table must be considered in its preparation. This includes the centering of the titles and column headings, and precise intersection of lines to form neat corners.

TABLE 3-2. D STATEMENT PARAMETERS

CARD COLUMN	FIELD DESCRIPTION	VALUE(S)	SPECIFICATION RULES
1	Card Type	D	Always a constant "D".
3-8	Fieldname	axxxxx	The fieldname is a symbolic name given to the field being defined. It is coded left-justified and is from 1-6 alphabetic or numeric characters, of which the first character **must be** alphabetic. Special characters may **not** be used in a fieldname. Within a given file definition, each fieldname must be unique. Any field or part of a field may be defined as many times with as many names and attributes as required. See Appendix B for a list of reserved names.
		ƀƀƀƀƀP	For a repeated field entry, following the data definition D card for the first element of the group, enter the special data name, ƀƀƀƀƀP. See section 3.6.

FIGURE 5-2. Table Example (Reprinted with permission of TSI International Ltd.)

TABLE 3-2. D STATEMENT PARAMETERS (CONT.)

CARD COLUMN	FIELD DESCRIPTION	VALUE(S)	SPECIFICATION RULES
9-12	Field Displacement	0000-8192	This parameter specifies the displacement of the leftmost byte of the field being defined from the beginning of the logical record. The first position on a record has a displacement of 0000, **not** 0001. The Field Displacement parameter must always be numeric and leading zeros must be coded.
			For ISAM unblocked files, the key field must be defined as the first n positions of the record (0000 to n-1) where n is the length of the full key. For example, if an ISAM unblocked file had a key length of 12, then the first field on the file would have a displacement of 0012, **not** 0000.
			For variable-length records, except VSAM, the first field on the file would have a displacement of 0004 **not** 0000.

FIGURE 5-2. (continued)

TABLE 3-2. D STATEMENT PARAMETERS (CONT.)

CARD COLUMN	FIELD DESCRIPTION	VALUE(S)	SPECIFICATION RULES
			For bit-string data ("X" in Field Type), the displacement of the bit is the byte in which the bit appears.
			For half-byte data ("L" or "R" in Field Type), the displacement of the half-byte is the byte in which the first half-byte starts. Refer to section 3.5.
13-16	Field Length	0001-0256	The field length parameter specifies the actual length in bytes of the data on the logical record.
			For bit-string data ("X" in Field Type), this parameter contains the relative position of the bit within the byte, from 0001 (leftmost bit) to 0008 (rightmost bit).
			For half-byte data ("L" or "R" in Field Type), this parameter contains the number of half-bytes being defined.
17	Field Type		This parameter specifies the mode in which the field being defined is stored on

FIGURE 5-2. (continued)

TABLE 3–2. D STATEMENT PARAMETERS (CONT.)

CARD COLUMN	FIELD DESCRIPTION	VALUE(S)	SPECIFICATION RULES
			the record. The following are the allowable Field Types:
		C	**Character or external form (EBCDIC).**
		P	**Packed decimal with standard sign conventions.**
		B	**Binary signed numbers. The length for fields defined as binary can be either 1, 2, 3 or 4 bytes only.**
		X	**Bit definition.** This field type allows for the definition of individual binary bits. The data is considered by the SORT and Print Phase as though it were a number with the value 0 or 1. X field types may not be periodic.
		L/R	**Half-bytes.** This value indicates whether the field being defined starts in the L (Left) or R (Right) half-byte of a byte. Refer to section 3.5. L/R field types may not be periodic.

FIGURE 5-2. (continued)

TABLE 3-2. D STATEMENT PARAMETERS (CONT.)

CARD COLUMN	FIELD DESCRIPTION	VALUE(S)	SPECIFICATION RULES
18	Alphanumeric/ Numeric Indicator	A	This value defines a field as containing alphanumeric data. The length of an "A" type field may be from 1-256 bytes.
			Any field type may be defined as an "A" type field (i.e., a field can be defined as CA, PA, BA, XA, LA, or RA). However, only those defined as CA should be used in an Extract Phase ENTER statement. All others (PA, BA, XA, LA, and RA) should only appear in the Print Phase or SORT statement.

FIGURE 5-2. (continued)

5.1.8 Using Illustrations

Illustrations supplement the manual text, emphasizing the technical content. Their use permits a writer to expand the text for the reader's benefit. For this reason, they should not be taken lightly. In addition, they make your job easier and break up the manual text, adding variety to straight narration. The use of one effective illustration in a mass of technical material might spark that one bit of understanding for which your reader is looking.

They can range from simple flowcharts consisting of several logic symbols, to a complex flowchart covering several pages. In addition, halftones (photography) of technical equipment or terminal keyboards might be used to supplement the text, or anything that you feel could be important in creating an effective manual. The number and types of illustrations are limitless; however, ensure that they are prepared by an artist capable of professional work.

If computer printouts are used in the text as illustrations, they should be reduced to fit within the margins. Then have the artist draw neat lines around the reduced printouts to make them stand out.

All artwork must be given to the artist in the early stages of a manual's development. Refer to Chapters 3 and 8 for information concerning preliminary artwork.

5.1.9 Using Key Letters to Explain Data and Coding

Explaining congested data and coding may seem a tedious prospect. However, each type of explanation can be approached in almost similar ways. Two approaches are invaluable in explaining a great deal of complex material. The end result will benefit the reader and allow him or her to digest the technical data more easily.

EXPLANATION OF CONGESTED DATA

Often, areas of information are congested in one spot, such as the entries on an output report. A simple method of identifying the entries and linking them to a narrative explanation is through the use of key letters.

The key letters (A-Z, AA-ZZ, etc. for as many entries as are on the report) must be shown on the report example. They must, for instance, be in a bold face and circled. A line with an arrow should be shown extended from the circled letter to the appropriate entry. The entries, in turn, will be identified in the text with the associated key letters and explanations. Refer to Figure 5-3 for an example of the explanation of data on an output report using key letters.

This approach is very useful in explaining technical data on a highly complicated report. The flexibility of the lettering scheme proves itself continually.

In addition, if the need arose, this type of approach could be used to explain input (forms, cards, etc.) or other types of output. Its application provides a neat method of presenting data that is simple to reference, an asset to both the reader and writer.

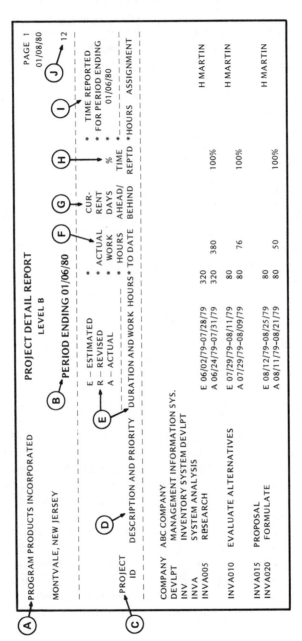

FIGURE 5-3. Explanation of Data Using Key Letters (Reprinted with permission of TSI International Ltd.)

Code	Task		Schedule	Est	Act	Var	%	Hrs	Assigned
INVA 025	PRESENTATION	E	08/26/79–09/02/79	16					
		A	08/22/79–09/02/79	16	20		100%		H MARTIN
INVA030	MODIFICATIONS	E	08/26/79–09/03/79	40					
		A	08/26/79–09/02/79	40	33		100%		H MARTIN
INVA035	DESIGN								
INVA040	REPORT LAYOUTS	E	09/09/79–09/28/79	120					
		A	09/03/79–09/29/79	120	140		100%		R JOHNSON
INVA045	DATA BASE								
INVA050	RECORD LAYOUTS	E	09/08/79–10/05/79	160					
		A	09/03/79–10/11/79	160	200		100%		H MARTIN
INVA055	RECORD RELATIONSHIPS	E	10/05/79–10/23/79	200					
		A	10/11/79–10/25/79	200	190		100%		H MARTIN
INVA060	D. B. DOCUMENTATION	E	10/27/79–11/25/79	160					
		R	10/27/79–12/30/79	160	125	-21	78%	40.0	H MARTIN
		A	10/26/79–						A FOSTER
								40.0	
INVA065	PROGRAM SPECIFICATIONS								
INVA070	PROGRAMS DEFINED								
INVA075	INPUT LAYOUTS	1	E 10/05/79–10/16/79	100					
			A 10/11/79–10/19/79	100	87		100%		R JOHNSON
INVA080	EDITING TO PERFORM	2	E 10/19/79–11/13/79	150					
			R 10/19/79–01/03/80	150				8.0	R JOHNSON

FIGURE 5-3. (continued)

Those fields identified on the Project Detail Report with letters A—J are as follows:

LETTER KEY	FIELD	DESCRIPTION
A	(name of company) (address)	— Identifies the company for which the report is being produced and its address.
B	PERIOD ENDING (date in MM/DD/YY format)	— Indicates the last date from which the project information will be included in this report.
C	PROJECT ID	— Identifies individual projects with a seven-position alphanumeric field.
D	DESCRIPTION AND PRIORITY	— Provides a unique description of the individual projects in a heirarchical structure.
		A two-digit priority number can be generated for each project, if desired. High priority items should be assigned lower integer values (e.g., priority 1). A default priority of 50 is assigned if no priority is entered.
E	E—ESTIMATED R—REVISED A—ACTUAL _____ DURATION AND WORK HOURS	— Provides a listing of start dates, end dates, and time estimates for each project. These dates can be the original estimate (E), a revised estimate (R), or the actual start and stop date (A).

FIGURE 5-3. (continued)

LETTER KEY	FIELD	DESCRIPTION
		E indicates the original project estimate, if entered. This estimate is retained even if it is later revised.
		R indicates a revision. The last R estimate is the current estimate of the project. The report can list up to eight R estimates per project. If further revisions are made, the eighth R estimate will reflect this revision.
		A indicates the project start date, if reported. If the project has been reported as completed, the completion date will be shown.
F	ACTUAL WORK HOURS TO DATE	— Is the actual time that has been reported on the project.
G	CURRENT DAYS AHEAD/BEHIND	— Indicates the current or projected days ahead or behind on the project.
	or	
	PROJECTED DAYS AHEAD/BEHIND	*A blank space* indicates that the project has no time reported or is not fully estimated.
		0 indicates the project is on schedule.
		? indicates the time reported exceeds the time estimate.

FIGURE 5-3. (continued)

LETTER KEY	FIELD	DESCRIPTION
		+ or – (figure) indicates the following: + is generated with a figure for days ahead of schedule; – is generated with a figure for days behind schedule.
		The current days calculation is the difference in days of the actual project status versus the project status required for on-time completion.
		The projected days calculation projects a completion date based on the rate of work completion to date. The difference of this projected completion date and the estimated end date is the "days ahead or behind."
H	% TIME REPTD	— Reflects the percentage of time reported by dividing the project estimate into the actual hours reported. Asterisks in this column indicate that more hours have been reported than the project estimate.

FIGURE 5-3. (continued)

LETTER KEY	FIELD	DESCRIPTION
I	TIME REPORTED FOR PERIOD ENDING (date in MM/DD/YY format)	— Is the current period ending date.
	HOURS ASSIGNMENT	HOURS shows the hours reported by the employee to the immediate right for the current period ending date.
		ASSIGNMENT lists the employee identification of employees assigned to a project. Multiple assignments can be shown.
J	(report number)	— Indicates the sequential number of the report out of the 47 that can be generated.

FIGURE 5-3. (continued)

DEFINING LINES OF CODING

Using a slightly different approach, lines of coding could be defined with information on the same page. The coding should be situated on the left-hand side; its definition on the right-hand side. An arrow will extend from the definition to the coding. The coding should be set according to standards; for example, in a ten point bold typeface. The definition should be in a smaller medium typeface. Refer to Figure 5-4 for a simplified example of this technique.

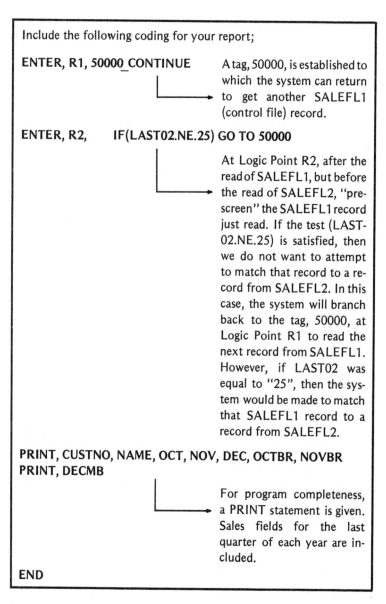

Include the following coding for your report;

ENTER, R1, 50000_CONTINUE

A tag, 50000, is established to which the system can return to get another SALEFL1 (control file) record.

ENTER, R2,   IF(LAST02.NE.25) GO TO 50000

At Logic Point R2, after the read of SALEFL1, but before the read of SALEFL2, "pre-screen" the SALEFL1 record just read. If the test (LAST-02.NE.25) is satisfied, then we do not want to attempt to match that record to a record from SALEFL2. In this case, the system will branch back to the tag, 50000, at Logic Point R1 to read the next record from SALEFL1. However, if LAST02 was equal to "25", then the system would be made to match that SALEFL1 record to a record from SALEFL2.

PRINT, CUSTNO, NAME, OCT, NOV, DEC, OCTBR, NOVBR PRINT, DECMB

For program completeness, a PRINT statement is given. Sales fields for the last quarter of each year are included.

END

FIGURE 5-4. Defining Lines of Coding Example
(Reprinted with permission of TSI International Ltd.)

This technique is very useful in explaining technically intricate data on a step-by-step basis.

5.1.10 Formulating Appendices

Appendices are often the catch-all for anybody attempting to write a manual. They are considered a convenient area to dump all technical material that does not fit into the text. This attitude is wrong. Appendices have a purpose, and as such, are a vital part of any manual.

They are a convenient means of isolating technical data that cannot be used in the manual text effectively, or is too lengthy, complicated or detailed. Appendices are unique and should be restricted to material such as calculations, formulas, extensive flowcharts and involved listings that would make the manual text awkward.

Appendices are effective in streamlining the text and making it easier for the reader to understand the material. In addition, the involved technical data is isolated into convenient modules that can be accessed directly. In this manner, they can be maintained more easily by the writer. Therefore, data would not have to be extracted from the text if a maintenance situation did arise.

Of course, certain guidelines should be observed when preparing an appendix:

- Each appendix must be identified and titled as outlined in the detailed manual standards. For example:

```
APPENDIX A
TECHNICAL CALCULATIONS
```

- If an appendix contains a table for simplification, it must be identified and titled as other tables in the manual, adhering to the detailed manual standards.

```
TABLE A-1.
PROGRAMS AND THEIR INTERRELATIONSHIP
```

In addition, the table should be prepared according to the guidelines in Subsection 5.1.7. As in a numbered chapter, a table will take the designation of its appendix and use it in conjunction with its sequential number. If the table is the first one in Appendix A, it would be designated "Table A-1."

- Do not use the letter designations "G" or "I." "G" is used in the page numbering scheme of the glossary. "I" is used in the page numbering scheme of the index.
- Error and system messages, their explanation, system action, and user action should not be placed in an appendix. They deserve more prominence in a separate chapter.
- Any graphic techniques that could be employed to enhance an appendix should be used. This could include such things as using different versions of the same typefaces to highlight some data (bold, italic, etc.). Another technique is leaving empty space around an item you are highlighting that is centered on the page. This could be a particular formula or coding that is part of a small but intricate textual explanation.
- Bear in mind that appendices are flexible. They can contain anything that is technically unmanageable in the manual text, but requires presentation. Use them wisely and only when necessary.

5.1.11 Preparing Front Tables

Front tables are essential to any type of publication that is printed. In the case of technical, user or installation manuals, it is imperative that they be prepared with some thought by the writer. The basic objective of the front tables is to direct the reader quickly to the main areas of information in the manual. The index, on the other hand, is designed to direct the reader to more specific areas of information. In both instances, a basic need of the reader is fulfilled.

Normally a table of contents identifies the chapters by number and title, in addition to the pages on which they begin. Also, the individual sections within chapters and subsections within sections are listed by number and title with their respective pages.

If the manual contains illustrations, a list of illustrations follows the table of contents on a separate page. All illustrations are listed sequentially from the beginning of the manual, with their respective figure numbers and the pages on which they are found.

If the manual contains tables, a list of tables follows the list of illustrations on a separate page. All tables are listed sequentially from the beginning of the manual, with their respective table numbers and the pages on which they are found.

Often a manual may contain a limited number of illustrations and tables. When this occurs, the list of illustrations and list of tables may be placed on the same page, thereby saving space.

When preparing front tables, specific attention should be given to the detailed manual standards shown in Section 3.2. These specific rules should be observed for titles, headings, typesetting, indentation of areas of information, and layout.

Bear in mind that the table of contents is the reflection of your detailed outline. Therefore, if the outline has been completed fully and organized well by you, the table will be quite simple to prepare.

5.1.12 Preparing an Index

The preparation of an index requires time and persistence; luxuries which most people do not have. There are different methods of producing an index; however, over the years I have developed a fairly efficient procedure to isolate the more specific areas of information to formulate an index. Its basic simplicity can provide you with the means to prepare one. Refer to Figure 3-7 for an example of an index.

Of course, an index cannot be started until the manual is typeset and paginated. In addition, the front tables should be completed. With the final typeset manual before you, you are ready to compile the index.

The initial transfer of information from the manual should be done using blank cards. You may wonder why cards are used rather than jotting the information on paper. Eventually, all the information must be alphabetized for the index; if the information were on paper, this would be difficult. By using cards, each unit of information can be juggled around until it is in the proper alphabetic sequence. Then all that is required is to transfer the information from the cards to paper in the proper typed format and give this to the typesetter who should know the index format (as defined in the detailed manual standards). If not, transfer the information from the cards to paper in the proper format and give this to the typesetter.

Basically the extraction of specific areas of information from the manual is quite simple, if you know the contents. Isolate the very general headings of information initially. Then isolate each succeeding subheading to the most specific until you have compiled all the necessary heading information. This may require your going through each chapter of the manual several times for each level of information.

For example, the first pass through a manual will give you the chapter headings, their section and subsection headings, and their associated pages. *Remember, place each title and page number on an individual blank card.* It should appear as:

System overview, 2-1

On your second pass through the manual, extract more specific areas of information and the associated page numbers. Continue this process for each additional pass through the manual until you are sure that all pertinent areas of information have been identified.

To make your index as complete as possible, try to cross-reference as many areas as possible as you go through. This procedure refines your index a little more, making it precise and a better reference guide for the reader. For example, the index might have an entry called "Files" with the names of all files and their associated pages listed under it. In the index, it might appear as follows under "F":

F

Files
    account master, 3-7, 3-20, 3-40, 3-99
    account transactions, 2-3
    closed accounts, 3-74, 3-75
    mortgage master, 3-5, 4-35
    savings account balance, 3-33, 3-54
    savings master, 3-5, 3-11

Now, each of these files would appear in the index by itself under its appropriate alphabetic identifier. For example, under "A," the following files beginning with the letter "A" would appear:

A

Account Master File, 3-7, 3-20, 3-40, 3-99
Account Transactions File, 2-3

Cross-referencing information is very important to the reader. It provides a certain flexibility that can assist the reader in looking for information.

When preparing a final index, you should establish and observe standards such as:

- Have your index consist of two columns on a page in the final typeset copy.
- The identifying letter of the group of entries should be centered over it and be in a bold typeface to stand out.
- If an entry has the same definition as another entry in the index, refer the reader to the other entry as follows:

BIZPST-*see* Savings Detail Program

The word "see" in every case should be in italics.

- Often, an entry may have additional information listed under it in the manual text or an associated illustration. In this case, ensure this information is listed under the entry alphabetically and in small letters. For example:

Backup run, 2-5, 3-13
    clerical input, 3-13
    clerical output, 3-13
    frequency, 3-15
    processing, 3-21
    program objective, 3-22
    special instructions, 3-23

---

or

> Extraction Control Report, 2-5, 3-32
> example of, 4-5

- If a letter has no entries, leave this letter out of your index. For example, if the letter "T" is left out, that portion of the index would appear as:

> **S**
>
> Savings Account File, 3-25, 3-44
> Supervisor responsibilities, 4-2, 4-25
> System overview, 2-1
>   program identification, 2-5
>   work flow, 2-1
>
> **U**
>
> User codes, 3-99
> Utility programs, 6-5

The preparation of an index for a technical or installation manual is essential. A user manual, however, may or may not need an index. It is an instructional book and may not require the quick reference to specific areas of information. This reference is established through the table of contents, which lists the functional sections. However, this need should be determined by the writer, who should have a strong picture of the user audience by this time.

5.2 UNIQUE TECHNICAL MANUAL TRAITS

In addition to the general procedures necessary in writing all types of manuals, technical manuals have certain traits that user and installation manuals do not have, one of which is a different writing style and terminology. Also, job control language (JCL) and related code should be highlighted, an effective technique that can isolate key areas of data for the reader.

5.2.1 Writing Style and Terminology

Technical manuals require a simple, direct writing style, one that can carry the reader through the text smoothly. In addition, all terminology must be the same throughout the text, for the benefit of the reader. For example, if you called a file the "Transactions File" in Chapter 1, refer to it as the "Transactions File" whenever it appears in the manual text. In general, technical people tend to change the file name or anything of a technical nature throughout the life of a system. It is imperative, therefore, that the writer be aware of this problem, and maintain consistency from the start of a writing project through to the end.

Besides consistent terminology, the general language of a manual requires simple words and phrasing. If something can be said in one word rather than six, use it. Simplicity is a quality that distinguishes good manuals from average ones. It is to your benefit to avoid the verbose language prevalent in many manuals today.

This view of writing can be carried to the other manual types, particularly installation manuals which in essence are a type of technical manual. User manuals, however, require a distinct writing style and terminology because of their nature.

5.2.2 JCL and Related Code

A necessary part of any technical manual is the JCL and coding that is instrumental in the operation of any system. As such, it must be presented in such a way as to catch the reader's eye. What would be the best manner of integrating it with the manual text? If it is dropped into the narrative, you may disrupt the flow you are trying to establish. Therefore, see how each particular coding would fit into the narrative; analyze its impact on the surrounding information.

Faced with the problem of introducing large segments of coding in a narrative, isolate each as an illustration and reference it in the text.

If you are explaining small segments of coding throughout the manual, it is much easier to leave it in the narrative, thereby maintaining continuity in the information flow. However, keep the coding as minimal as possible, i.e., one to ten lines.

NOTE: Refer to Subsection 5.1.9 dealing with the coding explanation. The use of arrows extending from the areas of explanation to involved coding is very effective.

When presenting any sort of JCL or coding, think of the reader. The clearer and neater coding appears, the better appearance your manual will have. To this end, plan how it will appear in the manual. This problem can be approached in two ways:

- Use the output from a printer.
- Have the typesetter typeset the final JCL or coding.

The easiest manner of presentation is to use the output from a computer printer. However, to use it as final artwork in the manual, certain precautions should be taken:

- The final typed copy must be proofread, ensuring that the proper columnar positioning from line to line is maintained. Width values of characters and numbers are the same, so no alignment problem occurs as with typeset copy.
- Use plain white paper in the printer. If this is not possible, have the computer operator reverse the normal line paper to the blank white side.
- Ensure a new ribbon is used on the printer, preferably a one-time carbon-coated ribbon.

The end result should be satisfactory for your final draft reproduction. The key to success is dark-printed copy on a white background that can reproduce well.

Or, the typesetter can take your copy and typeset each line of code. However, several problems exist even though the end result will be much better than computer-produced copy:

- The final typeset copy must be proofread, ensuring that the proper columnar positioning is maintained from line to line.
- To accurately typeset lines of code is difficult. Typeset letters have different character widths. The problem arises when you try to line up lines of typeset code. The letters and numerals will not fall into the columns you originally designated.
- The entire procedure is very time-consuming.

If the JCL or coding is typeset, it should be in a bold typeface so it can stand out from the manual text. In addition, if the JCL or coding is small enough, center it on the page after being introduced in the text. Leave enough open space around it.

Present day phototypesetting systems have the ability to interface with computers. Code that is in memory can be accessed and exactly produced as typeset copy. However, sufficient time must be spent with your company's technicians to ensure that all equipment is compatible. *All technical issues must be resolved.*

5.3   UNIQUE USER MANUAL TRAITS

User manuals are unique in the manual family. Although the general procedures for writing a manual apply, user manuals must be developed in a totally different light, showing a concern for the reader's environmental needs. The traits peculiar to them include a different writing style and terminology, and on-line system functional explanations.

5.3.1 Writing Style and Terminology

This aspect of user manuals is probably their most unique feature. The manual text is directed at the reader. It defines those functional steps necessary to utilize the technical data defined in the technical and installation manuals. In other words, the user manual is an instructional publication; however, technical detail must never be overlooked. Although it does not go into a system in great depth, the user manual must still contain sufficient information for reference purposes.

With a functional manual such as this, adhere to the following guidelines in its preparation:

- Give explanations one step at a time, when describing the steps necessary in performing a function. Of course, the functional steps must be introduced by narrative explaining the particular function and its interrelationship with the system.
- Express each individual step in the imperative mood. This is very important in that you are directing the reader to

do something. Try not to deviate from this rule unless you are explaining some particular point as part of the step. For example:

---

1. Enter the necessary information via the XYZ input card to obtain a listing of the COBOL program.

2. Enter the 1—5 character record type name in the data base.

    NOTE: The system will read the first record of this type in the data base.

- To save the wearisome repetition of steps, direct the reader to the initial statement of the same steps and indicate if they are in the same section or another section. For example:

---

5. Repeat steps 1—4 of this section.

---

or

---

5. Repeat steps 1—4 of Section 3.2 to continue processing.

- Use consistent terminology throughout the manual so as not to confuse the reader. For example, if a file was referred to as "Transactions File" in Chapter 1, refer to it as "Transactions File" whenever it appears in the manual text.
- Use simple words and phrasing as you explain a particular function. If something can be expressed simply without getting verbose, do so. Gear your writing for the person having the least understanding of the subject.

As you get involved more deeply in writing a user manual, you will find this approach to be very effective. Its application on a consistent basis will avoid complications in the preparation of user data.

NOTE: Bear in mind that a user manual still requires the same original research and preparation as a technical or installation manual.

5.3.2 On-Line System Explanations

To effectively describe the functional areas of information in an on-line system, it is necessary to depart from the normal steps taken to develop a user manual, because of the specialized requirements of some users. If your explanations of a particular function will involve terminal screens and keyboards, then ensure that illustrations of them are included. This is a prime opportunity to use illustrations in your manual, a technique that was described earlier. It is designed to amplify the narrative and place it in its proper perspective.

Introduction to this area of writing may seem difficult; however, once into it, the preparation of the functional explanation will become easier. Once the proposed user manual has been broken into the functional areas (through a detailed outline) and the necessary information gathered, the preparation of the manual can begin. After the general introduction in the first chapter, describe the basic system in the second chapter with an overview. Include a drawing or halftone of a terminal keyboard with which the user will key in information to the system. The keyboard should be clear, and all lettering on the keys visible. If necessary, provide any explanatory material concerning the keyboard. Your art department will be able to help you with this piece of art. The artist can tell you whether a photograph and a halftone made from that photograph is necessary, or a drawing should be made.

Prior to each function being explained, each screen to be displayed must be described in an earlier chapter. It is similar to the procedures explained in Subsection 5.1.9. In this case, you are describing a terminal screen rather than a report or input form; however, the same type of format is maintained in the narrative explanation. Refer to Figure 5-5 for an example.

2.2.5 REPORT DISPLAY/PRINT SCREEN

The Report Display/Print Screen is used to perform the following.

1. To display a report at the terminal.
2. To submit a report for printing.
3. To delete a report.

NOTE: These actions apply after a report request has been executed and the report is available in the terminal's library. If the request created more than one report, all are treated as a group under a common Report ID.

In addition, the Report Display/Print Screen may be used to perform the following.

1. To display a report request.
2. To display the FORTRAN source statements for the program that executed the report request.

Refer to Figure 2-5 below for an illustration of a Report Display/Print Screen.

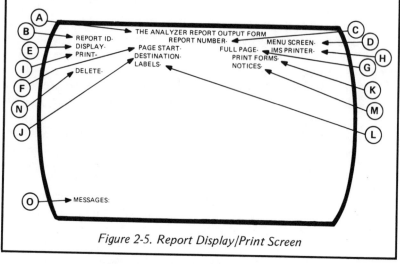

Figure 2-5. Report Display/Print Screen

FIGURE 5-5. Terminal Screen Description
(Reprinted with permission of TSI International Ltd.)

Those fields identified on the Report Display/Print Screen with letters A-O are as follows.

LETTER KEY	FIELD	EXPLANATION
A	THE ANALYZER REPORT OUTPUT FORM	— Identifies the terminal screen format.
B	REPORT ID-	— Identifies the report with a 1-8 character name or identification code. This name was assigned when the report was submitted for execution. It is one of the following.

1. The name was assigned by the user if the request specified that it should be saved in the terminal's library.
2. The name was assigned by the system and displayed as the Report ID in the MESSAGE section after the user pressed the ENTER key to submit the request.

NOTE: Do not enter the name of a report request. When the objective is to display the statements in a request, the system will use the report name and display the request with which it is associated.

FIGURE 5-5. (continued)

LETTER KEY	FIELD	EXPLANATION
		If the request defined more than one report, the same name applies to all of them. They will be treated as a group for printing, display, or deletion.
C	REPORT NUMBER-	— Identifies the report which is to be displayed on the screen with a 2-digit report number. It may be left blank for report #1, language analysis, or a FORTRAN listing.
D	MENU SCREEN	— Allows the user to return to the Master Menu Screen. This is done when the user types "X" or any other character in this field and presses the ENTER key. **NOTE:** The system will ignore any other codes on the screen.
E	DISPLAY-	— Allows a user to display a report at the terminal. This is done when the user types "Y". **NOTE:** This field must be left blank when printing or deleting a report.

FIGURE 5-5. (continued)

LETTER KEY	FIELD	EXPLANATION
F	PAGE START-	— Indicates the page at which the report will start or any associated display/printing activity where

blank= when displaying a report at the terminal and you want to start at page 1,

001-999= when displaying a report at the terminal and you want to start at a page other than page 1. For example, key in 045, to start the display at page 45,

REQ= to display The Analyzer's report request statements that were used to create a report,

CMP= to display the FORTRAN language source statements for the program that actually produced the report,

LBL= to display the LABEL Macro output, and

NTC= to display the NOTICE Macro output.

NOTE: Ignore this field when submitting a report for printing.

FIGURE 5-5. (continued)

LETTER KEY	FIELD	EXPLANATION
G	FULL PAGE-	— Allows a user to perform one of two options on the terminal screen where **Y=** two terminal screen lines are used for each print line in the report. (The first 79 characters appear in the first screen line; the remaining 53 characters are in the second line.) and **blank=** the screen shows one line for each print line. (The display includes only the first 79 characters in each line.)
H	IMS PRINTER-	— Allows a user to produce a report on the IMS printer associated with the terminal. This is done by entering the 8-character LTERM name. Only reports will print here.
I	PRINT-	— Allows a report to be printed on a high speed printer in the central data center unless another printer is specified in the DESTINATION field (letter key J). This is done by entering any nonblank character. **NOTE:** This field is ignored unless the DISPLAY field (letter key E) is blank.

FIGURE 5-5. (continued)

LETTER KEY	FIELD	EXPLANATION
J	DESTINATION-	— Is an optional field that allows a user to identify a remote station printer where a report can be routed. This is done by entering its 1-8 character name.
		NOTE: This field should be left blank when using a central data center printer.
K	PRINT FORMS-	— Is an optional field that allows a user to enter a forms code of up to 16 characters.
		NOTE: The system inserts this code into the output job control language for the print operation and supplies enclosing parentheses.
L	LABELS-	— Is an optional field that allows a user to enter a LABELS form code of up to 16 characters.
		NOTE: The system inserts this code into the output job control language for the print operation and supplies enclosing parentheses.
M	NOTICES-	— Is an optional field that allows a user to enter a NOTICES form code of up to 16 characters.

FIGURE 5-5. (continued)

LETTER KEY	FIELD	EXPLANATION
		NOTE: The system inserts this code into the output job control language for the print operation and supplies enclosing parentheses.
N	DELETE-	— Allows a user to delete a report from the terminal's library. This is done by entering any nonblank character.
		NOTE: This field is ignored unless the DISPLAY field (letter key E) and PRINT field (letter key I) are blank. If a printing or display action has been requested, do not delete a report until the print step has been completed.
O	MESSAGES:	— Displays certain status and error messages. Refer to Table 8-1 for a listing.

FIGURE 5-5. (continued)

Using the writing style discussed earlier, describe each function step-by-step. In addition, place a sample of a terminal screen display in strategic areas throughout the manual text. This technique is a good means of instructing the user in a particular function, showing the terminal screen display after the keys of a keyboard are pressed.

After an instructive step is stated, explanatory information can follow, if desired, in parentheses. Text information describing the function or general information can be used, following the normal paragraph structure.

To illustrate this approach, Figure 5-6 shows instructive steps, explanatory information, general text and terminal screens for a particular function.

When you identify the keys on the terminal keyboard, refer to the key by name. In the example shown in Figure 5-6, ENTER is shown on the key and is called the ENTER key in the text. Also, ensure that it is typeset in capital letters to make it stand out.

This type of format should be followed throughout each functional area. It is simple, direct, and carries the user through the entire function. If areas on a particular terminal screen need to be explained or shown to the user, an arrow should point to that area with the explanation off to the side, as shown in Figure 5-7.

7.1.1 DISPLAYING A REPORT AT A TERMINAL

To display a report at a terminal, proceed as follows.

1. Press the CLEAR key.

   (The screen will be cleared. Then the cursor will appear in the first position in the upper left-hand side of the screen.)

2. Type in /FOR OCCOØØP1

FIGURE 5-6. Explanation of a Function Using a Terminal Screen (Reprinted with permission of TSI International Ltd.)

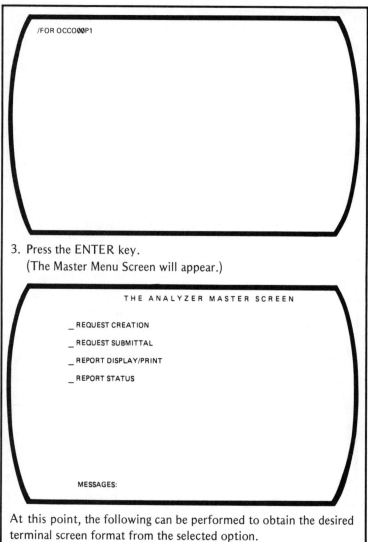

/FOR OCCO00P1

3. Press the ENTER key.
   (The Master Menu Screen will appear.)

THE ANALYZER MASTER SCREEN

_ REQUEST CREATION

_ REQUEST SUBMITTAL

_ REPORT DISPLAY/PRINT

_ REPORT STATUS

MESSAGES:

At this point, the following can be performed to obtain the desired
terminal screen format from the selected option.

4. Tab the cursor to the REPORT DISPLAY/PRINT option.

5. Type in "X" or any other character in the space to the left of the
   REPORT DISPLAY/PRINT option.

FIGURE 5-6. (continued)

```
            THE  ANALYZER  MASTER  SCREEN

  _ REQUEST CREATION

  _ REQUEST SUBMITTAL

  X REPORT DISPLAY/PRINT

  _ REPORT STATUS




  MESSAGES:
```

6. Press the ENTER key.

   (The system should switch to the Report Display/Print Screen. If there was an error, a message will appear at the bottom of the screen.)

NOTE: Any information that is initially displayed is installation-dependent.

```
                THE ANALYZER REPORT OUTPUT FORM
  REPORT ID-              REPORT NUMBER-          MENU SCREEN-
  DISPLAY-            PAGE START-         FULL PAGE-    IMS PRINTER-
  PRINT-             DESTINATION-          PRINT FORMS-
                     LABELS- A,,          NOTICES-
  DELETE-







  MESSAGES:
```

FIGURE 5-6. (continued)

NOTE: Refer to section 2.2.5 for a definition of the individual fields
on a Report Display/Print Screen.

7. Enter the 1-8 character name or identification code of the report
in the REPORT ID entry field.

NOTE: If the request defined more than one report, the same name
applies to all of them. They will be treated as a group for
printing, display, or deletion purposes.

8. Enter the 2-digit report number in the REPORT NUMBER entry
field to specify which report is to be displayed on the screen.

NOTE: The REPORT NUMBER entry field may be left blank for
report 1, report request, or FORTRAN output.

FIGURE 5-6. (continued)

```
                    THE ANALYZER REPORT OUTPUT FORM
    REPORT ID- LEE00001        REPORT NUMBER- 01        MENU SCREEN-
    DISPLAY-           PAGE START-          FULL PAGE-      IMS PRINTER-
    PRINT-             DESTINATION-            PRINT FORMS-
                       LABELS- A,,             NOTICES-
    DELETE-




    MESSAGES:
```

9. Enter "Y" in the DISPLAY entry field to display the report at the terminal.

```
                    THE ANALYZER REPORT OUTPUT FORM
    REPORT ID- LEE00001        REPORT NUMBER- 01        MENU SCREEN-
    DISPLAY- Y         PAGE START-          FULL PAGE-      IMS PRINTER-
    PRINT-             DESTINATION-            PRINT FORMS-
                       LABELS- A,,             NOTICES-
    DELETE-




    MESSAGES:
```

10. Enter "001-999" in the PAGE START entry field if you want to start the report at a page other than page one; otherwise, leave the field blank.

(The displayed page will be page one. For this example, the PAGE START entry field will be blank.)

FIGURE 5-6. (continued)

```
                THE ANALYZER REPORT OUTPUT FORM
     REPORT ID- LEE00001      REPORT NUMBER- 01        MENU SCREEN-
     DISPLAY- Y       PAGE START-          FULL PAGE-     IMS PRINTER-
     PRINT-           DESTINATION-         PRINT FORMS-
                      LABELS- A,,          NOTICES-
     DELETE-




     MESSAGES:
```

11. Enter "Y" in the FULL PAGE entry field or leave it blank where
    Y= Use two terminal screen lines for each print line in the report.
        (The first 79 characters appear in the first screen line;
        the remaining 53 characters are in the second line.) and
    blank= The screen shows one line for each print line. (The dis-
        play includes only the first 79 characters in each line.)

```
                THE ANALYZER REPORT OUTPUT FORM
     REPORT ID- LEE00001      REPORT NUMBER- 01        MENU SCREEN-
     DISPLAY- Y       PAGE START-          FULL PAGE-     IMS PRINTER-
     PRINT-           DESTINATION-         PRINT FORMS-
                      LABELS- A,,          NOTICES-
     DELETE-






     MESSAGES:
```

FIGURE 5-6. (continued)

12. Disregard all other entry fields on the screen.

13. Press the ENTER key.

(The page that you wanted displayed at the terminal will appear. When a report is displayed, a message at the bottom of the screen will advise users to press the PA1 key when there are additional pages.)

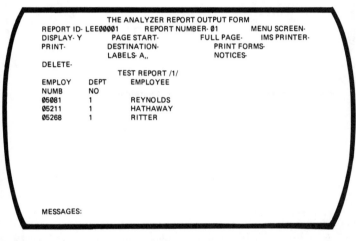

```
              THE ANALYZER REPORT OUTPUT FORM
   REPORT ID- LEE00001      REPORT NUMBER- 01      MENU SCREEN-
   DISPLAY- Y         PAGE START-         FULL PAGE-     IMS PRINTER-
   PRINT-            DESTINATION-          PRINT FORMS-
                     LABELS- A,,          NOTICES-
   DELETE-
                       TEST REPORT /1/
   EMPLOY     DEPT       EMPLOYEE
   NUMB       NO
   05081      1          REYNOLDS
   05211      1          HATHAWAY
   05268      1          RITTER




   MESSAGES:
```

NOTE: The system will display up to 16 lines at a time. It skips to a new screen for each new page of the report. The maximum number of screens for each report name varies from one installation to another. If there are more than 16 lines, the message "OCC0105 HIT/PA1/KEY FOR NEXT PAGE" will appear. If the report exceeds the number of installation-specified screens, the message "OCC0106 ENTER A/DISPLAY/ REQUEST FOR MORE OUTPUT" will appear at the bottom of the last screen displayed. At that point, move the cursor to the DISPLAY entry field, re-enter Y, and press the ENTER key.

FIGURE 5-6. (continued)

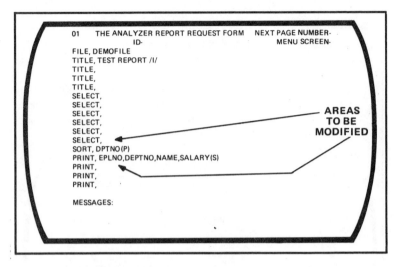

FIGURE 5-7. Identifying an Area on a Terminal Screen
(Reprinted with permission of TSI International Ltd.)

All system messages that could appear should be placed in the final chapter of the manual. All standards involved with preparing tables should be observed.

After your initial draft of the manual is completed and approved, the work of typesetting the text and preparing the screens must be done. If at all possible, try to finalize the information on the screens as early as possible and turn them over to the art department. The information must be typeset exactly as it is to appear on the screen.

Initially the art department should make one standard screen (approximately four inches high and five and one half inches wide) using a thick line. From this one screen, "stats" (reproducible copies) can be made and the typeset screen information placed on each copy. Then after all copies have been proofread and corrected, each screen can be reduced to fit into the space allocated in the typeset text (for instance, to approximately seventy-five percent of its original size). After the proper reduction percentage has been determined and the screens reduced (to approximately three inches high by four and one-eighth inches wide), the completed screens can be placed on the camera-ready page with the typeset copy by the artist. Note that with the reduction, the original thick line of the screen will be thinner but of excellent reproducible quality.

NOTE: Ensure that you give the artist the necessary specifications concerning the individual screens prior to finalization. This includes spacing between words, number of lines in each area of information, and how far the longest lines project to the left and right sides of the screen.

After all screens are completed, proofread the data on them letter by letter. Look at their overall layout. They must be as close as possible to their terminal screen counterparts.

Constant use of these techniques will increase your expertise in this area. With the increasing growth of on-line systems, their constant application will prove invaluable to those data processing professionals requiring clear and concise information.

5.4   UNIQUE INSTALLATION MANUAL TRAITS

Installation manuals are basically technical manuals with a slightly different approach. They must be written for technicians who must read the technical material in order to install and service a system. In that respect, they can be considered user manuals. The one trait that singles out this type of manual is its writing style and terminology. In addition, installation information can be presented in several ways, aside from a manual presentation. The proposed methods of presentation give you flexibility in the proper manner of presenting installation material. Consider each one and apply it to achieve the most effective results for your particular needs.

5.4.1 Writing Style and Terminology

Installation manuals require the simple, direct writing style found in technical manuals, one that can carry the reader through the text smoothly. Yet the manual text must be directed at the technician, giving the step-by-step procedures necessary for system installation.

As with all other manuals, terminology must be consistent throughout the text for the benefit of the reader. For example, if you called a file the "Transactions File" in Chapter 1, refer to it as the "Transactions File" whenever it appears in the manual text. In addition to consistent terminology, the general language of a manual requires simple words and phrasing. If something can be expressed simply without getting verbose, so much the better.

5.4.2 Multiple Units of Installation Documentation

The key to preparing an installation manual is *organization*. Without it, you will create a complex situation, one in which different types of information cannot be communicated properly. Some of it consists of large blocks of data; others consist of short sections that stand alone. To integrate all of this information into a workable unit necessitates a thorough understanding of the documented technical data and the needs of the personnel installing the system. The manual must be geared to their unique environment.

Installation documentation can be presented in a typical manual format, maintaining all the rules of organization and writing previously discussed. Usually a manual format is the choice of presentation because the information is part of a large block of description that defines several key topics. It is the simplest and easiest way to attack the problem.

But often, installation documentation covers a broad spectrum of topics, all of which are an integral part of the installation of a system. With the myriad of technical documents that must evolve, the problem for the writer could prove to be monumental. The situation has always been complex and probably always will be. In addition to the basic manual format, installation documentation can be presented in the following ways, if individual units of information must be prepared:

NOTE: It must be stressed that the requirements of the people using the information must be studied before a specific method is used.

- *Prepare each unit of information as a separate entity.* Each unit of information can be prepared individually as a small manual, pamphlet, or one or two page write-up. The trouble with this type of approach is:

  − Loss of control if the number of units of information becomes excessive.
  − Too many pieces of documentation to coordinate with the printer.
  − Storage problems.
  − Excessive involvement of time and manpower.

  If, however, this course of action is to be taken, ensure that each unit of information, even if it is not in a manual format, adheres to some basic standards. Maintain these standards and consistency in writing and terminology.

  With a little effort and determination, you may be able to overcome the drawback of this approach. Plan it out before you get involved, and compare it to the other approaches for multiple units of installation documentation.

- *Place units of installation documentation in a special folder.* This approach to installation documentation is easier on you, as all printing and assembling is done by a printer. However, it will be more costly because the individual units are assembled in a specially designed folder as shown in Figure 5-8.

  By placing your material in a folder such as this, you solve the problem of control; everything is under one cover. In addition, the inside flaps could be used as a table of contents to list the various pieces of installation information.

- *Separate units of installation documentation into individually designed file folders which, in turn, would be placed in a specially designed enclosure.* This approach is, of course, the most expensive as far as printing and assembling costs are concerned; however it is the most attractive and practical of the approaches.

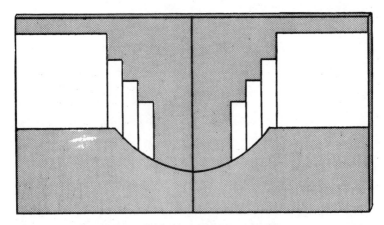

FIGURE 5-8. Use of a Special Folder for Installation Documentation

Figure 5-9 demonstrates how the separated units of installation documentation are placed in a folder. The file folders are easily accessible; thus the user need not shuffle through the individual units of information for what he needs. Everything is there. In addition, there is a great deal of open space on the inside cover, which could be used for a table of contents listing the various sections of information, and an outside cover for marketing purposes.

This approach is geared for the writer, allowing the preparation of individual units of data in an organized manner.

Whether you prepare an installation manual or assemble individual units of installation documentation in one of the three approaches mentioned, do it with the following thoughts in mind:

- Follow a basic set of standards.
- Follow a detailed outline.
- In your writing, think of the person installing the system and consider his needs.

Each point is essential to produce installation material effectively and avoid the pitfalls that might appear.

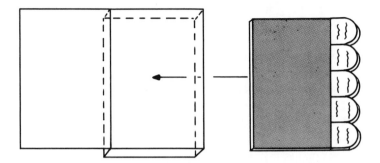

FIGURE 5-9. Use of Individual File Folders in an Enclosure

5.5   PROCEDURE MANUALS

A procedure manual is significantly different in format from those manuals previously discussed; however, it is linked to other manuals in one respect. The written material must be organized in a logical sequence from beginning to end. In addition, it must be geared for the reader who must use the data on a continuing basis. Within this framework, two areas of information must be covered in each procedure of the manual:

- Procedure definition.
- Functional responsibilities of each person involved.

These areas of information must be developed within a set of standards designed specifically for a procedure manual. Bear in mind, however, that various phases in a manual's development parallel those of the technical, user and installation manuals. To avoid confusion, therefore, this section covers the procedure manual from its inception to its inevitable maintenance. Eight significant steps are described, emphasizing certain concepts. Each logically takes the writer through the manual's development.

- Developing a format for individual procedures.
- Defining a procedure.

- Defining the functional responsibilities.
- Using tables.
- Using illustrations.
- Reviewing individual procedures.
- Developing a manual format to contain individual procedures.
- Maintaining procedures.

5.5.1 Developing a Procedure Format

Initially a format must be developed for individual procedures, one which facilitates their integration into a manual in a logical sequence for its reader. The standardized structure necessary must be developed around a specific "form," which can be used to define a procedure and its associated functional responsibilities. Refer to Figure 5-10 for an example of a procedure form that could be used.

To accomodate procedural information, the body of the form is blank. On the top left-hand side, a company logo should be placed. Adjacent to it is space for the procedure title, code number and effective date of the procedure. On the bottom of the page is the revision number and page number. These items of information are common to each page used for an individual procedure. They are defined as follows:

- PROCEDURE NAME. Identifies the procedure in concise language. It should be typed in upper and lowercase letters.
- NO. The code number of the procedure. It provides ease of reference within the procedural format, identifying each procedure numerically, and its associated department within a company. For example, the first procedure of a systems development department could be coded SD-0001. Then additional procedures could be numbered sequentially.
- EFFECTIVE DATE. Identifies the date when the procedure should be observed by the responsible people.
- REVISION__. Identifies the status of the procedure.
- PAGE__OF__. Identifies a specific page and the total number of pages in the procedure (e.g., PAGE 1 of 7, PAGE 2 of 7).

| COMPANY LOGO | PROCEDURE NAME _____ |
| | NO. _____ EFFECTIVE DATE _____ |

REVISION____   PAGE__OF__

FIGURE 5-10. Procedure Form Example

A procedure should be written using this form in two ways:

- As a cover page, containing data pertinent to the life of the procedure.
- As pages which contain the actual procedural data.

COVER PAGE

The cover page of a procedure should contain the following areas of information (from top to bottom) after the standard identification data and effective date:

- Approval signatures, titles and dates.
- List of Effective Pages for the procedure (i.e., revision numbers of pages and their dates).
- Distribution list and number of copies.

The information on the cover page provides enough information to effectively maintain a procedure. It covers all phases in the life of a procedure from its approval to its distribution and eventual maintenance. Refer to Figure 5-11 for an example of a typical cover page.

PAGE(S) CONTAINING PROCEDURAL DATA

The second and succeeding pages of a procedure should contain the following areas of information (from top to bottom) after the standard identification data and effective date:

- Procedure definition.
- Individual functional responsibilities.
- Optional illustrations and tables to enhance the procedure.

These pages should provide all information necessary to understand a procedure and perform the individual functions for its successful conclusion. Each section of information should be treated as a modular unit. Individual functional responsibilities, for example, should not be placed on the same page. This is necessary to allow for ease of maintenance in the future. Refer to Figure 5-12 for a basic example of typical pages containing procedural data.

COMPANY LOGO	PROCEDURE NAME Writing Functional Specifications
	NO. SD-0001 EFFECTIVE DATE 2 FEB. 81

This procedure has been studied and approved for distribution.

_____ _____ _____ _____
(signature and title)   (date)   (signature and title)   (date)

LIST OF EFFECTIVE PAGES

Page 1-3   Original - 2 Feb. 81
Page 4-5   Change 1-5 March 81
Page 6   Original - 2 Feb. 81
Page 7-10   Change 1-5 March 81

DISTRIBUTION

Quality Assurance - 2 copies
Systems Development - 3 copies

REVISION____

PAGE 1 OF 10

FIGURE 5-11. Typical Cover Page for a Procedure

A. PROCEDURE DEFINITION

This procedure will define those steps necessary to plan, organize, and develop functional specifications to be used in system design.

Sections of the functional specifications will be prepared by individual System Analysts and submitted to the Project Manager for final preparation.

FIGURE 5-12. Typical Procedure Data Page

B. SYSTEM ANALYST (GRADE 1)
    RESPONSIBILITIES

The System Analyst (Grade 1) must define the system for the functional specifications as follows:

1. Expand on the areas of information outlined in the basic project plan.
2. Identify features and future enhancements.
3. Indicate if the system will affect any other software products currently produced by the company.
4. Put all data in the established format and forward it to the Project Manager for review.

FIGURE 5-12. (continued)

C. PROJECT MANAGER'S RESPONSIBILITIES

The Project Manager must coordinate all sections of the proposed functional specifications. To do this, proceed as follows.

1. Place data received from all System Analysts in the established format.
2. Submit the first draft of the functional specifications for review to the pertinent department heads.
3. After receiving any comments, enter them and have copies of the functional specifications printed.
4. Distribute the functional specifications to all members of the Systems Development Department who are involved in the system design.

FIGURE 5-12. (continued)

5.5.2 Defining a Procedure

A procedure is defined on the second page (as shown in Figure 5-12) of a procedural write-up and should normally be restricted to that page. Its purpose is to introduce a particular procedure to the reader. For the benefit of the reader and the writer, the definition must be written clearly and convey enough information to explain the procedure in basic terms.

In this definition, all functions necessary to complete the procedure must be shown. In addition, all interrelationships between functions must be described in general terms. Further detailed information can be explained in the sections involving individual functional responsibilities.

Bear in mind that the same writing techniques used for technical, user and installation manuals must be applied.

5.5.3 Defining Functional Responsibilities

Definition of functional responsibilities in a procedure gives the reader an insight into what each job requires. It also allows the reader to see how the different functions tie together for the successful completion of the procedure. Refer to Figure 5-12 for a typical page defining a functional responsibility.

The functions involved and the steps necessary to complete them must follow a logical sequence. The description of a person's functional responsibilities must expand on the procedural definition. All detail must be given.

When defining functional responsibilities, certain rules should be observed:

- Keep each section of functional responsibilities as a separate unit (i.e., start each functional responsibilities section on a new page).
- Write clearly and simply.
- Use the imperative mood in a step-by-step explanation.
- Use illustrations to highlight sections of text, if necessary. If a detailed section of text is difficult to explain, an illustration might be used (e.g., a simple flowchart).
- Use tables if a great deal of technical data must be incorporated into your explanation.

When a section outlining the responsibilities of a particular function nears completion, ensure that the information flows logically into the next functional responsibilities section. Develop an interrelationship between the two distinct functions. For example, consider the last step of a "Programmer's Responsibilities" section to be the following:

```
7. Ensure that the computer listing detailing
   the coding for (program name) are given
   to your Project Manager by 5 P.M. daily.
```

Then the next functional responsibilities section for the Project Manager might begin:

```
After receiving the computer listings detailing
the coding for (program name) from the pro-
grammer, proceed as follows.
```

By writing a procedure using this technique, the writer is able to carry the flow of work from section to section.

5.5.4 Using Tables

Tables can be used in a procedural write-up as effectively as in a technical, user or installation manual. The distillation of technical data into concise blocks of information that can be referenced easily should be considered when the occasion arises. Your objective in writing individual procedures is to present the information in such a manner as to assist the reader in the performance of his or her function. If it is feasible, therefore, use tables frequently to condense complex data into an easy-to-reference format.

In summary, those criteria for tables stated in Subsection 5.1.7 should be observed with minor modifications as follows:

- The identifying number and title of the table must be centered over the table; however, the table numbering scheme of a procedure manual deviates from the standards in Section

3.2 due to its unique nature. The numbering scheme should be restricted to a numeric sequence (e.g., TABLE 1, TABLE 2) for each procedure.

- Columnar headings need only be typed in upper and lower-case letters and centered, if desired. Horizontal lines will separate the headings from the information.

5.5.5 Using Illustrations

As in the technical, user and installation manuals, illustrations supplement the text, being used to emphasize key areas of information for the reader. For example, when explaining the responsibilities of a programmer, it might be necessary to illustrate the work flow of his or her particular function, as shown in Figure 5-13.

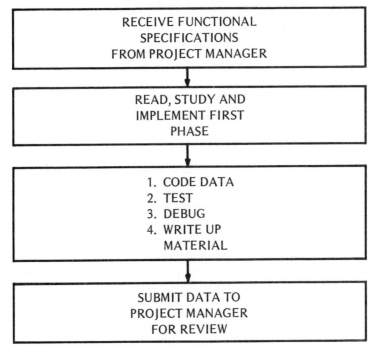

FIGURE 5-13. Sample Work Flow Illustration

Procedural illustrations, for the most part, should be simple because of the size of a typical procedure. Common illustrations that might also be used include uncomplicated flow charts, layouts of terminal keyboards, computer printouts (reduced to fit in the text), or forms that must be completed as part of a function.

5.5.6 Reviewing Individual Procedures

After each procedure is written and typed, submit it for approval with the standardized cover page. Usually only one review per procedure is necessary due to its small size. As a procedure is signed and dated by an individual, he or she should pass it to the next person whose name appears on the cover page. In essence, the person is verifying that the procedure has been studied, is correct, and can be distributed. If an item in the procedure is wrong, the correction should be noted on a separate sheet of paper and returned to you with the typed procedure. After corrections have been made, the procedure can be resubmitted to the proper reviewers for their signatures.

When the procedure is finally approved and the cover page signed, have the necessary copies of the procedure made and distribute them.

NOTE: In all reviews, the writer should emphasize the need for a complete study of the proposed steps to make sure the procedure works. This can avoid problems which could occur at a later date.

5.5.7 Developing a Manual Format to Contain Individual Procedures

Once a format for individual procedures has been developed, reviewed and implemented, thought must be given to a manual format. It must be simple and easily maintainable, for the writer's benefit and the convenience of the reader.

Basically a procedure manual should be divided into sections, each of which contains a set of procedures for departments within a company that have a working relationship with its data processing facility. In addition, a section should exist for those procedures of a general nature which would apply to all departments. In turn, these sections should be placed in alphabetic order using the two letters of the procedure code number. For example, a company may consist of the following departments, each having its own set of procedures with assigned procedure code numbers:

- Personnel (PR)
- Marketing (MA)
- Auditing (AU)
- Systems Development (SD)
- Software Research (SR)

If you followed the aforementioned guidelines, each set of procedures for the company would be organized as follows:

- Auditing (AU)
- General (GN)*
- Marketing (MA)
- Personnel (PR)
- Systems Development (SD)
- Software Research (SR)

Within each section, the procedures would be placed in the proper numeric sequence (e.g., SD-0001, SD-0002, SD-0003 for the Systems Development Department). Then a "section" table of contents must be prepared for each section rather than a "manual" table of contents. This approach is practical for a procedure manual because of the maintenance problem. The table of contents must contain all code numbers, procedure names and effective dates. An example of a section table of contents is shown in Figure 5-14.

Constant updating of the table of contents is essential when new procedures and changes are written. If the table of contents and procedural data is not kept up to date, the procedure manual will lose its value.

*This section contains general procedures for all personnel.

TABLE OF CONTENTS (SYSTEMS DEVELOPMENT)		
PROCEDURE NO.	PROCEDURE NAME	EFFECTIVE DATE
SD-0001	Writing Functional Specifications	20 Feb. 81
SD-0002	Writing System Specifications	3 April 81
SD-0003	Using the XYZ Terminal for Coding Purposes	1 May 81
SD-0004	Preparing the Monthly ABC Report	1 May 81

FIGURE 5-14. Section Table of Contents Example

When completed, the individual set of procedures should be separated by dividers, each of which identifies the data by department name and the first two letters of the procedure number. For example:

```
SYSTEMS DEVELOPMENT
       (SD)
```

Each tab on a divider should have a plastic covering. In addition, these dividers should have a plastic covering running along the edge where the three holes are situated. The plastic covering in both areas saves wear and tear on the dividers.

Finally all procedures should be placed in a three-hole binder. It should be large enough to accomodate existing procedures and have significant room for future growth.

5.5.8 Maintaining Procedures

On occasion, a procedure may require maintenance because of changes in the daily operation between a department and the data processing facility. When this occurs, it is necessary to make changes to the procedure quickly to avoid any interruption in the data processing work flow. Of course, the appropriate personnel should be made aware of the changes to the procedure to facilitate its introduction to the daily work routine.

Basically the routine that should be followed in procedure maintenance consists of four basic steps:

- *Isolating changes.* This function is usually initiated by the department causing the procedural change. If this is the case, discuss the situation with the appropriate staff members to obtain the correct information. Also, find out when the change will take effect. The following should be observed to achieve a firm grasp of the upcoming change:

  - The manner in which the procedural text will change and to what degree.
  - The effect of the changes on the physical structure of the procedure, particularly on the increase and decrease of the pages.
  - Verification of the technical content of the changes by management and the technical staff.

  After these points have been clarified and all changes organized in a logical sequence, their actual insertion in the text can be performed.

- *Entering changes in the text.* Excluding entire new pages that are added, place neat black lines in the outer margin of the corrected pages opposite the changed areas. This identifying mark will allow the reader visually to identify corrections on the revised pages. In conjunction with the black line, the current revision number must be placed in the lower left-hand corner of the changed page; the effective date will be in the upper right-hand corner.

  Entire pages that have been changed will be clearly identified with the current revision number and effective date. They need not have a black line in the outer margin.

- *Completing an inventory of current pages in the affected procedure.* As part of the cover page, a list of effective pages must be prepared. Its purpose is to serve as an inventory sheet listing all the pages, their revision status, and effective dates. Refer to Figure 5-11 for an example of a cover page containing this information.

- *Printing and distributing change pages.* After approval of changes by the appropriate staff members, printing of the change pages should be initiated. Eventually the proper number of copies will be distributed to those departments listed on the cover page. Refer to Figure 5-11 for an example of a cover page containing this information.

CHAPTER SIX

The Review Cycle

Technical, typographical and grammatical accuracy, organization and clarity must be integrated into the text of every manual. To achieve this goal, the following steps must be taken.

- Definite review procedures must be established for the appropriate members of the technical and marketing staffs.
- The individual procedures must be presented to the reviewers in a standardized format and kept current.
- Management must provide the support necessary to enforce a prescribed review cycle. Without this support, you fight a losing cause.

An objective review is highly desirable to obtain a more complete publication. To this end, the prosepective user should be asked to review the forthcoming manual. This will:

- Provide a close examination of the data and manual format from the user's point of view.
- Promote effective public relations between your company and the prospective user.

To simplify the explanation of the review cycle, this chapter is divided into two sections: review procedure for manuals, and proofreading.

Section 6.1 discusses particular review procedures for draft copies of manuals, including the individual review phases in the development of the documentation. Section 6.2 deals with proofreading. This aspect of the review cycle is particularly important to the writer who must face typographical errors and poor grammatical structure on a daily basis. It provides a positive answer to a problem that continually plagues him or her.

6.1   REVIEW PROCEDURE FOR MANUALS

The time at which a manual is reviewed is based on its life cycle, which should have been developed when work first started on the project. If you remember, there are five phases in a life cycle:

- Initial preparation and organization (Phase 1).
- Writing and draft reviews (Phase 2).
- Typesetting and typeset draft review (Phase 3).
- Final writer verification (Phase 4).
- Printing (Phase 5).

For purposes of this review procedure, concern yourself with two of these phases: 2 (initial rough, working and preliminary draft review), and 4 (final writer verification). If all reviewers and users do their jobs with dedication, there need not be any other drafts prepared. The unique opportunity to obtain users views could result in a manual geared to the needs of the marketplace.

Common to each review is the sign-off sheet, an important document that is useful to you, the person responsible for the manual being reviewed. A sign-off sheet can take any form. The main thing is that each staff reviewer must sign and date it. As each draft copy of the manual is developed, the sign-off sheet should be attached and delivered with a copy to each staff member for review.

The sign-off sheet should contain certain information prior to the reviewer getting the manual copy:

- Identification of the manual.
- Date the manual is given to the reviewer.
- Date when the manual must be returned to the writer.
- Whether the manual copy is the initial rough draft, working draft or preliminary draft.
- Any pertinent information that the reviewer should know (e.g., whether the manual is incomplete, or has a missing chapter or section of information that will be issued shortly).

In turn, the staff reviewer must enter certain information on the sign-off sheet:

- His or her signature in the space provided.
- The date of the signature.

To assist you in visualizing such a form, refer to Figure 6-1 for a sample sign-off sheet. The sample shown is typed on half of a letter-size sheet of paper. It can be reproduced as you need it.

The use of this form is important to you and the company. It is a small but integral part of the life cycle of a manual. As such, it should be developed for use in a documentation organization of any kind. It serves a twofold purpose:

- Providing an accurate tally of reviews of the individual drafts.
- Giving you signed proof that a certain manual was reviewed on a certain date by a particular person.

NOTE: Always keep the signed sign-off sheet in a locked filing or storage cabinet. Of course, the pertinent drafts containing all comments or lack of comments should be stored also.

MANUAL TO BE	DATE
REVIEWED _____	ISSUED _____
Initial	DATE TO BE
Rough ☐ Working ☐ Preliminary ☐	RETURNED
Draft Draft Draft	TO WRITER _____

This draft of the aforementioned manual is technically correct as far as I can determine. Changes and/or corrected information have been placed in the attached draft copy.

_____   _____
(Signature of Reviewer)   (Date)

FIGURE 6-1. Sign-off Sheet

6.1.1 Initial Rough Draft Review

This area of review, by its very nature, produces the most comments and changes by your reviewers. The draft is prepared from rough technical data and interviews. Thus, some data may have been overlooked or is incorrect. Different reviewers look at the initial rough draft differently, based on their unique experience, knowledge, interests and viewpoints.

At this point, the initial rough draft should not be reviewed by a user, because it is still in the process of being prepared. It is suggested that the user review the working and/or preliminary drafts only. However, this approach can be altered to fit your company's needs.

Each reviewer should represent a segment of your company that has some interest in the manual. Ideally the people who helped you gain information for the manual should be included. This way, all technical bases are covered. Of course there is management to consider, but that is later on in another review stage. Right now, worry about the organization and technical accuracy of the manual.

Prior to distributing the initial rough draft, ensure that it is typed neatly and double-spaced to allow for corrections either through conventional means or a word processing facility. In addition, ensure that the rough artwork is included in the appropriate areas. The draft should be organizationally correct and as close to being a complete copy as possible. With a respectable initial rough draft that meets strict standards of organization and neatness, the reviewer can judge the technical material more accurately.

Then, ensure that the proper number of copies are run off. Attach a sign-off sheet to each copy, enter the appropriate information, and submit the copies for review. While the draft copies are being reviewed, review the manual yourself to ensure that its organizational structure follows your outline, information flows, continuity is maintained and standards followed. In addition, check for typographical errors, misspellings and mistakes in grammar.

Any comments you make should be placed in a master copy of the initial rough draft. When you receive comments from the staff, incorporate them in the master copy also. If the comments are not reasonable or there is a conflict, get the matter resolved by going to the individuals involved.

All reviewer comments should be placed in their draft copies in red ink or some other contrasting color. This is important because you have to interpret the comments and transpose them to your master copy. If they were written in black pencil or pen, they might be overlooked.

Also, emphasize to all reviewers that the text of the draft must physically be changed on their copy. They should not question an area and then disregard it, leaving the writer to provide the proper text. If not, they should at least take the initiative and direct you to the proper people for assistance, or show you where the correct information can be found. Nothing is more frustrating than finding comments in a reviewer's draft copy like, "Why is this so?" "This isn't right," and "What is the reason for this remark?" It is the reviewer's obligation to answer the question or at least provide the proper direction. The writer has enough problems with which to contend; researching a reviewer's question need not be one of them.

On the initial rough draft, ensure that everything is explained that might be questionable, such as the use of boldface type or text indentation. In addition, when you bring the draft copy for correction, explain all of the manual's requirements to the typist. This saves you trouble at a later time. Of course, he or she should have a set of standards in which all these requirements are explained.

While the initial rough draft is being retyped, set aside all the reviewed copies and sign-off sheets in a safe place. You will assemble more copies from other reviews as time passes.

6.1.2 Working Draft Review

It is important in this second stage of review that the basic structure of the manual not be changed, a point that must be emphasized to reviewers. Comments to change the manual's organization should have been made in the early development of its life cycle.

The purpose of the working draft review is to correct any technical inaccuracies, enter any additional changes (so long as it does not affect the organization), and correct any misspellings or typographical errors. Any additional information to strengthen its accuracy must be entered at this point. This also includes constructive comments from selected users if they are reviewing the manual.

When you receive the working draft, ensure that the proper number of copies are run off and distributed. Each reviewer who reviewed the initial rough draft should review the working draft. In addition, appropriate levels of management should be given a copy to make them aware of the manual's appearance and general content.

At times, some constructive criticisms can evolve that might add to the manual's appeal. However, anything that might change any of the technical content should be examined carefully by the appropriate technical staff members.

Attach a sign-off sheet to each copy, enter the appropriate information, and submit the copies for review. While the draft copies are being reviewed, review the manual yourself to ensure that it was retyped as indicated in the initial rough draft, and proofread the text for typographical errors and misspellings.

All comments should be transcribed onto a master copy of the working draft. This includes your comments and those of all reviewers. If the comments are not reasonable or there is a conflict, get the matter cleared by going to the individuals involved.

Again, all reviewer comments should be placed in their draft copies in red ink or some other easily-seen color. Transposing them to your master copy will be easier.

On the master copy of the working draft, explain everything that might be questionable, and write legibly. A clear copy will speed up the turnaround time from the typist. This is particularly important with a tight time schedule. When the draft copy is finally brought to the typist for change or correction, explain the changes.

While the working draft is being changed and corrected, set aside all the reviewed copies and sign-off sheets in a safe place with those from the initial rough draft review.

6.1.3 Preliminary Draft Review

This last step of review is very critical. It represents the last opportunity for the staff to examine all technical material and correct any errors. Here again, the basic structure of the manual must not be changed and no major revisions made. However, you will find that someone always comes up with an urgent change that must get in the manual. Naturally you cannot refuse because the manual would be incorrect. *So, indicate the difficulty of correcting the manual at this time. This point should be emphasized for future publication development.*

When you receive the preliminary draft from the typist, ensure that the proper number of copies are run off. Each reviewer who received the working draft should review the preliminary draft. Again, the dissemination of drafts should now include the appropriate levels of management and selected users. Their input at this point in the review cycle should provide an indication of how the manual will be received. As with the technical staff, emphasize the difficulty of entering changes at this time to management.

Attach a sign-off sheet to each copy, enter the appropriate information, and submit the copies for review. While the draft copies are being reviewed, review the manual yourself to ensure that all corrections from the working draft were entered correctly.

In addition, check the areas where the corrections were made. Sometimes, in making corrections, the typist might have had to retype an area of information that contained the change. If so, that area of information could conceivably be in error and must be corrected. It is very easy to make an error in this manner. Check everything and verify its accuracy.

All comments made should be placed in a master copy of the preliminary draft. This includes your comments and those of the staff, management and users. If the comments are not reasonable or there is a conflict, get the matter cleared by going to the individuals involved.

Ensure that all review comments are placed in their draft copies in red ink or some other suitable color so that transposing them to your master copy will be easier. On the master copy of the preliminary draft, explain everything that might be questionable and write legibly. At this point, the manual is ready to be typeset.

Set aside all the reviewed copies and sign-off sheets in a safe place with those from the previous reviews. Ensure that they are enclosed in a box or suitable container and identified with all pertinent notes and data.

6.1.4 Final Writer Verification

This phase of the review cycle occurs after the manual is typeset and inspected by select members of management. It is the responsibility of the writer to ensure that the typeset copy follows the preliminary draft word for word and is grammatically correct.

As this is the typeset copy of the manual, all chapters, sections, tables and illustrations are firmly established. Therefore, pages can be numbered. When this is done, the table of contents, list of illustrations, and list of tables must be prepared followed by the index. When you bring the draft copy to the art department for any corrections (along with the table of contents, list of illustrations, list of tables and index), explain them to the typesetter and artist. Inform them of your page numbering scheme.

Finally when you receive the corrected typeset copy with page numbers, the table of contents, list of illustrations, list of tables and index from the art department, make a final check to ensure all corrections were entered. In addition, the newly typeset areas must be proofread carefully. *As a final step, go back through the text and verify all references.* If there are any errors, have them corrected.

When you are satisfied that everything is accurate, this last stage of review is over. The typeset copy of the manual is ready for the printer, being as technically and aesthetically correct as possible.

6.2   PROOFREADING

Proofreading is regarded as the most tedious aspect of any writer's job. Because of its very nature, it is avoided by many people and usually limited to only a cursory glance at the documentation. This is definitely the wrong approach in controlling the quality of a manual. It is to the writer's benefit to approach this task positively. A good job of proofreading is a final quality control procedure, geared to assist the writer in producing accurate manuals.

Proofreading is the actual verification of rendition accuracy, by comparing the original written or typed copy with the typeset or typed draft copy. All typographical errors and misspellings must be caught, along with any deviations from the established standards. To achieve this goal, proofreading requires dedication and a desire to produce a professional piece of documentation.

Even if an outstanding job of proofreading is done, there will still be errors in your manual. No matter how diligent a person is, something is always overlooked. However, most of the small errors can be picked up as well as the most blatant. To produce documentation that has few errors requires some systemization. The procedure offered here is not foolproof, but it provides you a base from which to start. With time, a concentrated program of proofreading can be formulated.

The proofreading aspect of your job appears in the draft reviews after a manual has been typed or typeset. Proofreading will also be done after the last draft review, when corrections are verified and the front matter and index completed. Each time, however, the proofreading can be formulated.

Initially allot yourself enough time to proofread your manual. *Time is the big factor.* To ensure that every letter and word is correct, you must move slowly. Remember, the eye only sees what it wants.

If possible, give a copy of the manual to another person to review who is not so technically-oriented. Familiarize him or her with your standards and explain the purpose of the manual. Emphasize that you want an objective review. He or she should particularly look for organizational flaws, typographical errors, grammatical errors and misspellings. A person in this position provides a different viewpoint that can be invaluable.

Besides this person's review, it is extremely important that you go through the typed or typeset material word for word. Compare each word to the initial rough draft or first draft with corrections, as the case may be. If necessary, place a straight edge under each line if the lines are close together. Here again, a great deal of time is spent but it is well worth the effort. Mark each error on your typed or typeset copy with a red pen and paperclip the page. If the error is minute, the typist or typesetter might overlook it when correcting the errors. The paperclip serves as a reminder.

After the other reviewer is done and you have completed proofreading, you are ready for the next step. Obtain the services of another person such as the production coordinator or another writer on your staff to assist you. First, find a place that is totally isolated, if possible. One person places the corrected typed or typeset draft in front of him or her, while the other person refers to the draft containing the written corrections. This person reads word for word to the person with the corrected typed or typeset draft, who notes any errors. When reading, the beginning of each paragraph and sentence must be verbally identified; each punctuation mark noted; and an indication made of any special typefaces, indentations or special conditions. This tedious process should be done in short spurts. To relieve the strain, switch off with the other person.

To reiterate, the important things that should be done in proofreading are:

- Have another person objectively read a typed or typeset copy of the manual in addition to the staff reviewers and selected users.
- Proofread the corrected manual yourself, cross-checking with the master copy having the written corrections.
- Verbally proofread the master copy of the manual with someone who checks the corrected typed or typeset copy.

If these three steps are taken, a manual will become a highly effective document, one that fulfills the user's needs. Bear in mind that this program of proofreading describes the most ideal conditions. Most proofreading efforts are not so detailed in the data processing community.

CHAPTER SEVEN

Manual Maintenance

At some point, any manual requires maintenance because of changes to a system's design or correction of any errors. When this occurs, it is necessary to effect the changes as quickly and smoothly as possible for the benefit of all those who read the manuals.

To perform maintenance on a manual, a certain routine should be followed prior to implementation of each series of changes. This routine must be performed in such a way as to sustain the manual standards that were initially developed. Of course, any maintenance to a manual is only as good as the standards that are written and, to a greater extent, enforced. The purpose of this chapter, therefore, is to outline a basic maintenance procedure for manuals using the standards that have been developed.

As improvements are designed into systems and errors found in previous designs, or just spelling and typographical errors, it becomes necessary to perform maintenance. Before this situation arises, the writer must develop a general routine to keep the manual as complete as possible, and not a patchwork quilt composed of odd pages and stray bits of information.

This type of approach is applicable for most types of manuals because they follow the same basic format. Manuals should be written as modular units, based on the standards proposed in Chapter 3. This writing approach effectively lends itself to the straightforward maintenance routine proposed here. It allows the writer to complete the job in an efficient manner within a reasonable time.

Basically the routine that should be followed in manual maintenance consists of four basic steps:

- Isolating changes.
- Entering changes in the text and typesetting.

- Completing an inventory of effective pages.
- Printing and distribution of change pages or the entire manual.

NOTE: If the manual is used as a selling tool, it might be necessary to redo the entire manual and repaginate it rather than issue change pages.

7.1 ISOLATING CHANGES

After a manual is initially published, a file should be established where corrections, additions, deletions and typographical errors from individual manuals are kept. The person submitting these changes to you should be identified and a date noted for your reference. When enough changes accumulate or when dictated by management, a revision to the manual can be initiated. By filing all changes, a great deal of time and manpower can be saved. To be effective, however, the file of changes must be kept current.

At the point when a revision to a manual is necessary and your change file is full, issue a memo to the technical staff. Indicate that a proposed revision is to be made to a particular system and requires changing all related manuals. Because of this, any further changes to the manuals must be sent to you by a certain date. Management should back you up in this regard to ensure the manual's swift revision. These initial formalities are necessary to make everyone aware of upcoming changes and the impact of these changes on the manuals and related technical documentation.

Changes should be submitted to you as clearly and completely as possible within the time frame you establish. As you get the comments, study them. Compare them to changes that you have already filed. Then check them against the areas which are to change in the manuals. As you go through the text, observe the following to achieve a firm grasp of the task facing you:

- *The manner in which the text will change and to what degree.* Initially look at the changes as a whole. What key areas will change technically and to what extent? How will these technical changes affect other critical areas directly and indirectly? These questions must be foremost in your mind as you consider the changes' impact on the readability of the manual.

- *The effect of the changes on the physical structure of the manual, particularly on the increase and decrease of pages.* Inevitably the introduction of changes will affect the physical structure of the manual. With the elimination of pages and the addition of new ones, your basic page numbering scheme and, possibly, section numbering scheme will become unworkable, thus affecting time and budget considerations. Therefore, it is necessary to plot out the entire maintenance routine. How will the changes affect the physical structure? What is the best way to lay out the revised manual? These questions must be answered.

- *The technical accuracy of the changes by management and applicable technical staff personnel.* Verifying this is an absolute necessity.

The clarification of the aforementioned points represents the first step in a writer's attempt to organize information, change the manual structure, and verify the validity of data. When this is done and all changes assimilated, ensure that the information is placed in a logical sequence. This is necessary as you approach the next step in the maintenance procedure, the actual writing and entering of changes in the basic manual text.

7.2   ENTERING CHANGES IN THE TEXT, AND TYPESETTING

Initially work with a spare copy of the current manual. Starting at the first page of text, go through entering all minor changes as they occur. If the changes require additional pages to be inserted, do so.

Write the additional text, ensuring it meets the manual standards you originally established and fits into the overall information flow of the manual. If the additional information falls in the middle of existing text, place an asterisk, letter or some other identifying symbol at that point. Then place the additional written information as closely as possible after that symbol on a separate sheet of paper. Ensure that the additional material has the same identifying symbol, to permit recognition.

On the other hand, if small segments of information on pages and whole pages have to be eliminated, do so. Cross out the areas that are no longer pertinent and extract those pages that are of no use. Do this as clearly as possible to avoid any problems for the typesetter. At this point, do not worry about the page numbers. They will be taken care of at the appropriate time.

Excluding the entire new pages that are added, place neat black lines in the outer margin of the appropriate pages opposite the changed areas. These identifying marks will allow the reader to identify corrections visually in the revised typeset copy. The new pages will be identified clearly by the maintenance page numbering scheme and therefore need no such identification. If these new pages had this black line, it would defeat your purpose of clarity, simplicity and neatness.

Those new pages that are added to a manual should be inserted between the appropriate existing pages and act as a conduit, providing a convenient flow of information. They will reflect all information that is pertinent to the revision of your manual. To show that they are new pages, a revision number and date will appear on the lower portion of each page opposite the new page number:

CHANGE 3–2 FEBRUARY 82

After all changes have been entered and all outdated information deleted, go through the text of the manual and ask yourself these questions:

- Did I change any sections that would drastically alter the initial outline of the manual?
- Did I deviate from the manual standards in any way?
- Does the new information blend in with the unchanged information and not disrupt continuity?
- Is the new information technically correct?

If you are satisfied with the answers and confident that all possible changes have been entered, you are ready for the next phase of maintenance: retypesetting.

After ensuring that the pages are in their proper sequence, place the rough draft of your revision aside in a folder. Then pull out the most current version of your manual's original camera-ready pages and place them in another folder. All camera-ready pages of all final typeset drafts should have been set aside in a locked cabinet, as stated earlier in this book. Ensure the rough draft pages are numbered sequentially for the typesetter on the back side of the page. They are only for his or her use at this point.

Take both versions of the manual to the art department or appropriate typesetting facility, and show the artist what has to be done. If he or she can salvage the most current camera-ready pages, so much the better. Perhaps only a few corrections have to be made to a page or, possibly, none at all. In any case, it is imperative you supply the artist with the camera-ready pages for this purpose.

When all new pages have been typeset and new information entered on existing camera-ready pages, the art department should return the revised manual to you for review. Run this revised typeset draft through the standard review cycle as outlined in Chapter 6. When the revised manual has been approved, you can correct the page numbering on the unchanged pages of the camera-ready copy. Then check the sequential continuity of all pages. If there are new pages, write the appropriate page numbers in light blue (nonreproducible) pencil where they are to go.

If new pages fall at the end of a portion of existing manual text, they will be numbered following the normal numbering sequence. For example, if the last page of a series is 2-10 and two new pages are added, they would be numbered 2-11 and 2-12.

However, if new pages fall between two existing pages, they will disrupt the pagination process, particularly when they are printed on both sides. If this occurs, certain conventions must be observed:

- *If the new information consists of an odd number of pages and falls between an even and odd page of existing manual text, the reverse side of the last page of new information will be blank and unnumbered.* For example, if three new pages are to be inserted between 5–4 and 5–5, they would be numbered 5–4a, 5–4b and 5–4c. The reverse of 5–4c would be blank. The next page on the right-hand side will be 5–5.

- *If the new information consists of an odd number of pages and falls between an odd and even page of existing manual text, the page following the last page of new information will be blank and unnumbered.* For example, if three new pages are to be inserted between 5–5 and 5–6, they would be numbered 5–5a, 5–5b and 5–5c. The reverse of 5–5 would be 5–5a. The page following 5–5c on the right-hand side would be blank. The reverse of this blank page would be 5–6.

- *If the new information consists of an even number of pages and falls between an odd and even page of existing manual text, that even page of existing manual text remains the same.* For example, if four new pages are to be inserted between 5–5 and 5–6, they would be numbered 5–5a, 5–5b, 5–5c and 5–5d. The reverse of 5–5d would be 5–6.

- *If the new information consists of an even number of pages and falls between an even and odd page of existing manual text, that odd page of existing manual text remains the same.* For example, if four pages are to be inserted between 5–4 and 5–5, they would be numbered 5–4a, 5–4b, 5–4c and 5–4d. The follwing page after 5–4d on the right-hand side would be 5–5.

NOTE: To understand these four conditions more fully, it is recommended that you actually insert sample pages in a manual as described in the preceding examples.

After the pagination process has been completed, the next step is to change the front tables to reflect the changes that were entered in the text. Make a copy of the front tables and place the necessary corrections on the appropriate pages. If whole pages of front tables are changed, rewrite them in longhand. Then set them aside. Repeat this process for the index.

At this point, you should have the following items for the art department:

- A camera-ready draft of the revised manual (with lightly penciled page numbers).
- A rough draft of the front tables.
- A rough draft of the index.

Now, using the front tables as a guide, go through the text of the manual and verify all references and the section, subsection, table and figure numbers. These numbers must check against each other, reflecting the changes that were entered. If they do not, indicate the changes lightly in pencil in the text and paperclip the pages.

After being assured that everything is correct, submit the camera-ready draft, front tables rough draft, and index rough draft to the art department or typesetting business. Any changes in the camera-ready pages and page numbers will be entered. In addition, the final drafts of the revised front tables and index will be done.

After receiving the material back, proofread everything that was done. Verify that the typesetter did, indeed, follow your instructions as far as page numbering was concerned. Use this final verification as the time to make one last inspection of the text. Ensure that the basic organizational structure of the manual was not altered, and there is a flow to the information that was added.

If everything has been done according to your instructions, set the revised camera-ready draft of the manual aside. One further step remains before you turn the manual over to the printer for printing, an inventory of effective pages.

7.3   COMPLETING AN INVENTORY OF EFFECTIVE PAGES

As part of the maintenance routine, it is necessary to list those pages that pertain to the new revision. To this end, a "List of Effective Pages" should be prepared and incorporated with the revised, new, and unchanged pages of the prepared camera-ready draft. Its purpose is to serve as an inventory sheet for all readers of the manual, listing all applicable pages and their dates of issue. At all times, the reader can check it to see whether a particular copy of a manual is current. It also serves as a reference point for the writer, allowing him to verify when certain changes were entered.

In preparing it, be as simple and concise as possible for the reader's benefit. To achieve this goal, the list of effective pages should indicate the following information:

- The total number of pages that are current in the manual.
- The individual page numbers, their change numbers, and the dates of issue for the change numbers. Original page numbers should also be included with their dates of issue and an indication of their "original" status.

For an example, refer to Figure 7-1.

LIST OF EFFECTIVE PAGES

NOTE: That portion of the text affected by the changes is identified by a vertical black line in the outer margins of the manual.

The total number of pages in (name of manual) is (number of pages), which consist of the following:

PAGE NUMBERS	CHANGE NUMBERS	DATE OF ISSUE
Title Page	Original	12 January 81
*i–iii	Change 1	14 June 81
*1-1–1-5	Change 1	14 June 81
1-6–1-7	Original	12 January 81
2-1–2-2	Original	12 January 81
*2-3	Change 1	14 June 81
2-4–2-12	Original	12 January 81

.
.
.

etc.

NOTE: The asterisk indicates pages changed, added or deleted by the new change.

FIGURE 7-1. List of Effective Pages Example

After the list of effective pages is finalized, typeset, printed and distributed with the change pages, the user can place it at the end of the manual to be referenced at a later time. Its use is particularly effective for manuals that have a large in-house use, such as different departments within a company which use a manual in the performance of their data processing functions. At any time, individuals in these departments can verify that their manuals are current, and confirm those pages affected by a change.

This page should, of course, be typeset as the rest of the manual. As changes are added to the manual and pages deleted with each revision, a new list of effective pages must be prepared. Its basic format is simple and provides a convenient vehicle to keep the reader advised of any change in the status of a manual.

7.4 PRINTING AND FINAL DISPOSITION OF CHANGE PAGES OR THE MANUAL

A decision must be made whether to reprint a manual completely or issue change pages to the user for insertion in a manual. In either case, a list of effective pages should accompany the change pages or manual in this final phase of the maintenance routine.

It should be noted at this point that certain factors concerning time and budget must be addressed by the writer before printing is done:

- Whether printing change pages or the entire manual, several quotes should be obtained from different printers to achieve a quality job at the best price. The writer/printer relationship is discussed in detail in Chapter 9.
- Ensure that sufficient quantities of sets of change pages or manuals are printed. Remember, ordering greater quantities saves your company money on a per unit basis.
- Plan the printing schedule with the selected printer well enough in advance so no time is lost in the delivery of the finished product. Keep the lines of communication open between yourself and the printer, if problems occur.

In addition, it is highly recommended that the individual sets of change pages be supported by a piece of cardboard and shrunk-wrapped in plastic sheeting by the printer. This covering protects each packet indefinitely, and at a nominal cost.

CHAPTER EIGHT

Artwork and Graphics
in Manuals

Throughout this book, many references have been made to artwork and its importance in explaining manual text, as well as the importance of a manual's exterior appearance in catching the user's eye. The aesthetic appeal of a manual in its entirety is so important that this chapter is devoted to several techniques that could be used by a writer. They range from the very subtle to the obvious. These techniques show that the information in manuals and related documentation can be presented effectively, even if the data is technical in nature. A departure from the traditional typed manual with lined drawings can be the answer to many of the problems faced by the writer today in attempting to capture the reader's interest.

This chapter addresses the following basic areas: text layout, effective typeface use, color for effect, and the criteria for the final reproduction copy. In addition, a section dealing with the relationship between the writer and artist and the proper lead time for the preparation of artwork is included. Each area of information (described in Sections 8.1 through 8.5) touches on the most common problems facing the writer, who may or may not be familiar with the intricacies of art and graphics.

8.1 TEXT LAYOUT

Before even starting to write a manual, you should have a firm idea of its tentative layout. Certain basic criteria should already be established in your detailed manual standards:

- Margins of a page.
- The basic modular structure of chapters, appendices, glossary, front matter, index and miscellaneous pages.
- Use of notes and cautionary information.

- Type sizes for the various section and subsection headings, figure identification, and table headings.
- Whether the pages of the manual should be printed on one or both sides.

Keeping these criteria in mind, a finer distinction of spacing between sections, subsections, figures and tables must be made. With the proper spacing, each significant area of information can stand out without special numbering or graphics. The slight difference between the spacing of two or four lines, for example, is amplified when the area of text is part of a long narrative in the manual.

After discussions with the artist and typesetter, come to some basic conclusions as to spacing when laying out manual pages. The main thing is that you establish certain spacing requirements to produce an appealing manual. Refer to Table 8-1 for suggested text spacing requirements.

The guidelines just mentioned can be changed, of course, based on your requirements. The information in Table 8-1 is not the answer

TABLE 8-1. Text Spacing Requirements

MANUAL AREAS OF TEXT	SPACING
Basic Areas of Text	
Between sections	Three lines—If at all possible, start each section at the top of a new page.
Between sections and subsections	Two lines—This spacing indicates a difference between the two areas, yet keeps them close enough to show an inter-relationship.
Between subsections	Two lines

TABLE 8-1. (continued)

Between manual text and the title of a table	Three lines—Allow three lines of space after the table as well.
Between the end of manual text and the beginning of a piece of artwork	Three lines—Allow two lines of space after the piece of artwork for the figure number and title, followed by three lines of space after which the manual text should begin.
Between each alphabetic grouping in the index	Three lines
Between each chapter listing and its sections and subsections in the table of contents	Two lines—Within each chapter listing, the sections and subsections follow one another with one line of spacing. Refer to Chapter 3 for an illustration of the spacing and indentation.
Between figure numbers and titles in the list of illustrations	line
Between table numbers and titles in the list of tables	line
Between paragraphs	Two lines

Major Headings and Basic Text

Between chapter heading and manual text	Three lines—The chapter heading should be centered at the top of the page.
Between the section heading and manual text	Two lines
Between the subsection heading and manual text	Two lines

TABLE 8-1. (continued)

All figure titles must be centered under the illustrations in the manual.

All table titles must be centered over the tables in the manual.

All column headings must be centered in a table in their appropriate columns. Enough room must be left for information to be put in the table in each column.

for every writer's particular situation. It is a conservative but effective way to lay out manual text using the best spacing techniques for maximum effect.

8.2 EFFECTIVE TYPEFACE USE

There are a multitude of typefaces that could be used in preparing a manual. The choice is clearly up to the writer and management.

Before typesetting begins, find out the different typefaces that are available with the equipment that the art department has. If you must have the manual typeset by a free-lance typesetter or company, find out the same information.

If possible, have a sample page of a manual typeset in the selected faces. It might be worth the expense to see what you are getting. If not, obtain a book of typeface samples, which your art department or typesetting company could supply. Then ensure that each echelon of management studies the various typefaces available to make selections. Remember, you will have to live with what is selected until the next reprinting of the manual.

Basically there are two categories of typefaces you can use in the main body of your manual: serif and sans serif. They are available in medium, bold and light. In addition, italic can be used in special circumstances. A serif letter has short lines stemming from and at an angle to the upper and lower ends of the strokes of a letter; for example: S. A sans serif letter has no such short lines; for example: S.

Selecting the serif and sans serif letter is strictly a matter of choice. I feel that certain serif typefaces lend a professional aura to a manual; on the other hand, some writers may say exactly the opposite. In any case, a decision should be made based on careful study, and your own likes and dislikes.

Once serif or sans serif is chosen, a specific typeface must be selected. The selection should be based again on careful study, and your own likes and dislikes. Study what is available with the equipment in your art department or outside graphics company. Suggestions from the artists in both areas will help you in this decision.

8.3   COLOR FOR EFFECT

Using color anywhere in a manual creates a problem: cost. Having two colors on a page (black being the other) multiplies the standard cost of printing a page considerably. Compare the cost when you receive estimates from the various printers to print your manuals. There is a decided difference.

Nonetheless, the contrast and appeal of color can dress up a manual, creating a positive impact on the reader. If color is used, it must not be overdone. The right amount of color in the correct areas can create a certain air of subtlety. On the other hand, too much color could create a garish piece of work that can be disastrous.

Some areas of a manual in which to use color, based on statements earlier in this book, are:

- Key letters and associated lines and arrowheads which point to data on an output report example or identify areas on a terminal screen (if an on-line system is being described) can be highlighted.
- Explanatory material for coding could be in a color to differentiate between it and the coding. This color should also be used on the line and arrowhead which point from the explanatory material to the coding.
- Key areas on selected pieces of artwork can be highlighted.

These areas are not the only ones in a manual in which color could be used. Your artist can assist you further in planning the use of color.

Often when using color, certain areas of a piece of artwork can be accented. In that case, a color can be screened (i.e., the basic color used is made lighter). Indicate to the printer that a certain percent screen is to be used in certain areas of the artwork. The higher percentage screen indicated (on a scale of 0–100%), the darker the color will be. For example, if you have a flow chart on which screening is to be used, provide the artist with appropriate instructions on the completed rough artwork (as shown in the example in Figure 8-1).

When selecting colors, consult your artist and printer. They are better equipped to select colors and have a better idea of how various colors will set on the paper stock selected for your manual. Some colors are extremely difficult to work with, such as whites, yellows and oranges. Darker colors, on the other hand, are easier to use. Bear in mind, however, that each color has its own unique problems, of which the printer is aware. With today's modern technology, colors

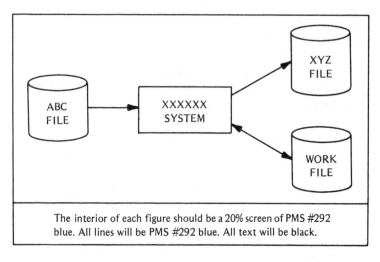

The interior of each figure should be a 20% screen of PMS #292 blue. All lines will be PMS #292 blue. All text will be black.

FIGURE 8-1. Instructions For Screening Artwork

are easier to use because of the effort employed by chemical ink manufacturers to make a better product.

In addition, ensure that any color chart from which colors are selected is no older than six months. Colors on the chart tend to fade after this period of time. When this happens, you may run into problems. The color selected from a chart that is over six months old may deviate from one that is used in the manual. Then after you receive the printed manuals, the color may not meet with your approval. *Therefore, be careful when using a chart.*

As with anything else in preparing a manual, select a color wisely. Study the various alternatives. Above all, get the approval of management for any major selection. A small amount of time spent in this manner will save you frustration in the end.

8.4 CRITERIA FOR FINAL REPRODUCTION COPY

Although you may not be involved directly in preparing the final reproduction copy for the printer, be aware of how a manual is to appear. In addition, be aware of what criteria should be used in its preparation. After all, the typeset copy of your manual represents the culmination of your work.

Up to this point, if you have developed your manual through its life cycle, you have prepared an initial rough draft, working draft, preliminary draft, and typeset copy (before corrections). Therefore, the final reproduction copy should be examined thoroughly to ensure all corrections were entered in the final typeset copy. It is a good idea to see the galley proofs of the copy before the final reproduction copy is produced.

As the writer, you should be aware of certain points about final reproduction copy. It can be finalized for the printer in two ways:

- The final copy can be typeset directly on letter-size high-grade paper which the printer will use in preparing the printed copy.
- The artist will paste up the typeset copy on a lightweight illustration board, producing a "mechanical."

In either case, all artwork must be interspersed between the text as needed; however, the artist has more flexibility with the copy pasted on the illustration board.

- The final reproduction copy is easier to handle.
- It can be preserved more easily over a longer period of time.
- Changes and corrections can usually be done in a short time.

Another added feature of copy on lightweight illustration board is that it can be protected by a thin transparent sheet of paper which is taped to the top of the board. When the printer uses the board in the printing of a page, this paper is flipped up exposing the camera-ready copy. When he or she is done, the paper comes down and covers the copy, protecting it from any accidental smudges or dirt marks. In addition, corrections can be written on this cover sheet during a review for the artist's use. Crop marks on each corner of the page should be drawn to assist the printer in lining up the page for negatives.

The only drawback with placing typeset copy on illustration board is that it takes longer to prepare. However, it represents an investment in producing a final reproduction copy that can be stored easily and will endure longer.

When you start to examine the final reproduction copy, spend a little extra time scrutinizing everything, down to the small dirt marks that are inevitably there. The cleaner you make the copy, the more professional a manual will be printed.

In addition, check the lines of type if you feel that they are crooked. There is nothing more disconcerting than a line of type that falls off at a slight angle. Even the most casual reader can pick it up and quickly tell you of its existence.

Finally ensure that all tables in the manual or any piece of art in which two lines join at an angle meet perfectly. Too often, the appearance of a good manual is hurt with lines that do not meet this criterion. It represents a small effort on the part of the artist to do this. If this occurs, inform the artist and have the lines corrected.

The outline of the irregular pieces of cut copy that are pasted on an illustration board will not appear on the final printed copy. These lines and any stray cut marks on the paper will disappear courtesy of the printer's skill.

8.5 RELATIONSHIP OF THE WRITER AND ARTIST

The relationship that a writer has to maintain with an artist can be fruitful if it is approached in the proper manner. If you deal with an outside artist, then you have nothing to worry about because it is strictly a business relationship. You do not have to worry about hurting his or her feelings or wondering what the status of your job is in comparison to others. Before the job begins, a completion date should be given you, to which you should hold the artist.

However, let's assume your company has an art department and a fairly competent artist with a supportive staff that consists of a paste-up person and one or two typesetters. You should have a good working relationship with each one of these people. A good idea would be to learn a little about each of their functions. Ask questions. They will be happy to help you. Of course, get the approval of their supervisor who, in all probability, is the artist.

The artist is the person through whom all work must be directed. As such, the rapport you develop will set the tone of your relationship for the balance of time you submit work to him.

In your initial dealings, be straightforward. Ensure that you explain your prospective manual to him or her in its early developmental stages. This way, the artist can adjust his or her work schedule accordingly for the arrival of the initial rough draft. Also, by knowing the complexity of the manual, the artist can make some rough calculations as far as time and labor are concerned, and give you a fairly accurate idea of when to expect the final product. Of course, as with anything else, difficulties can arise because of the personalities involved.

During this initial meeting, the artist can get a good idea of how much artwork is involved. So, have this part of your manual worked out before you see the artist. If you know that reductions will be involved or color is used, for example, it will be good to present these facts.

Preliminary artwork should be submitted to the art department in the early stages of a manual's development. This procedure helps you and the artist. It gets the artwork into production and out of your way. You can concentrate on the writing. The artist, in turn, can start to work on the artwork and finish it, hopefully, well in advance of the manual's due date.

With the artwork complete, the artist is not hampered when each page is being laid out. He or she knows exactly how much space is to be allocated between each grouping of text. Thus, time is saved and mistakes reduced.

In each phase of a writer's relationship with the artist, tact should be used but a firm hand applied. Insist on a professional job that does not deviate from your standards.

CHAPTER NINE

The Writer/Printer Relationship

During the development of a manual or other technical publication, a writer must inevitably deal with printers. This relationship is alien to most people, particularly the novice writer. Therefore, to enlighten the writer in this unique area of manual development, a basic understanding of certain information is necessary:

- The printing profession and some related technical areas.
- Printers as businessmen.
- The evaluation of good printers and their work.

Like anything else, your relationship with printers develops from a common understanding of each others problems and a mutual respect. As you deal with printers from job to job, you will develop an expertise both in your knowledge of the printing profession and dealing with this special breed of businessman.

To provide you with a base from which to develop this writer/printer relationship, nine major areas of information are discussed in Sections 9.1 through 9.9:

- Types of printers.
- Finding a printer.
- Determining a printer's capabilities and making a final decision.
- Receiving estimates on a job.
- Preparing a manual for a printer.
- Initial assessment of a printer.
- Long term assessment of a printer.
- The final printing process.
- Forms of binding.

When you complete reading this chapter, you should have a good idea of how to deal with printers. Constant writing, and dealing with them and associated vendors will gradually mold you into a highly qualified documentation specialist, a rare person in this data processing community in which we all work.

9.1 TYPES OF PRINTERS

The printing profession contains a multitude of printers doing different types of jobs. Some are so specialized that they limit themselves to one or two different specialties. For example, a printer could just print labels, wedding invitations, or do letterpress work. The list could go on and on because of the diversity of the printing trade.

For your purposes, an offset shop is required to print your manuals and any related technical documentation. The offset process is the most widely used in today's market and is the most economical in terms of a manual. It is a printing process in which an inked impression from a plate is first made on a rubber-blanketed cylinder on a press. Then the inked impression is transferred to the paper being printed. The plate never touches the paper; hence, the name "offset."

This offset process, therefore, is what you require from a shop with the necessary facilities. Those printers with which you might deal can be placed in three categories: instant printer, large-sized printer and medium-sized printer.

9.1.1 Instant Printer

This particular category should really not be classified as a printer. Instant printers are really people who came on the scene several years ago with copying facilities. They have simple offset duplicators which are really fast copiers, and a limited amount of reproducing equipment. Instant printers are also limited as to specialized jobs such as binding. Most of the time, they will just refuse the job. If one does take it, he or she will farm the job out to a specialist who can do it. You have seen instant printers in shopping centers or on the main street of your town with such names as "Quicky Service" or "Faster Than a Speeding Bullet Press."

An instant printer is probably good for short runs of a one-page item. Such a run is less expensive but costs more in the long run on a per unit basis. For this reason, instant printing attracts people off the street who need something right away, such as notices or circulars.

9.1.2 Large-Sized Printer

The large printers, who use the offset process and a multitude of other printing techniques, are geared for volume jobs. Their type of operation is one in which the owner does not usually associate with the customer directly because of the immensity of his or her dealings. The personal touch that is so necessary in dealing with the smaller companies is missing.

Normally the owner pushes the printing jobs through the salesmen. These salesmen deal with the customer and must try to get as much business as they can to obtain their commissions. They may or may not know the intricacies of the printing business. Therefore, the salesmen cannot offer the intimate service that you require. However, this may not be true in all cases. It depends on the owner of the printing firm and the standards he or she has set.

9.1.3 Medium-Sized Printer

The medium-sized printer is the one with whom you will probably work. It is in the medium-sized category that most printers fall. Of course, there are a mixture of competent and incompetent printers in this category.

One plus you have when you deal with a medium-sized printer, however, is that there is usually an owner-operator on the premises. Thus, the printer can usually deal with the customer directly, giving you better service. The printer is in a business that is highly competitive; therefore, he or she must do quality work.

A medium-sized printer can still be diversified, which is to your advantage. He or she usually specializes in black and white, or one to two-color jobs. In addition, this type of printer has the facility to do your entire manual from laying out the pages to binding the printed pages into a final product. Although this is true with a large-sized printer, you usually do not receive the intimacy that is so vital in a successful writer/printer relationship.

Within the medium-sized printer category, you will find printing concerns of varying sizes as far as personnel and equipment are concerned. Therefore, it is hard to describe the actual conditions necessary for a medium-sized shop. Your main concern should be the cooperation and service you require.

9.2   FINDING A PRINTER

At this point, you probably have decided on the type of printer to secure for the manual which you will publish. Now the job is to find a specific printer who can do the job.

The main problem is finding printers with whom you can talk. How should you approach this situation? Basically there are three methods of proceeding: by word of mouth, knowing a printer already, and using the yellow pages of the phone directory.

9.2.1 By Word of Mouth

This technique is probably the most common method of finding a good printer. Check with individuals in your company who have had printing jobs done. Find out if their jobs were acceptable and if the printers were easy to deal with. In addition, learn all the particulars about the printers before actually talking to them.

Normally the artist in your company's art department can provide you with direction. Also, check with the typesetter, who might have some ideas if he or she has been working in the business for some time.

Check with other departments within the company and ask the managers who might be in a position to help. If your company has an advertising or public relations department, direct your questions to this area.

Try other companies with which you have had dealings in the past. Through key personnel there, you should be able to find someone to whom you can talk. Even if you do not know anyone in another company, try talking to someone in that company's public relations or advertising department. The results might be productive.

Remember, you are looking for a quality printer, someone who will be recognized for a craftsman. His or her expertise and ability will be gratefully appreciated by the company for which he or she works. Eventually this fact will circulate. So, ask. You have nothing to lose and a printer to gain.

9.2.2 Knowing a Printer

You or management may have had some dealings with a printer in the past and been satisfied. Therefore, use this person, because you already have an idea of work he or she has done. However, this printer's capabilities must be restudied and the shop and personnel reevaluated. The printer may have changed in philosophy and work habits since he or she was last used. Evaluate your printer with the criteria discussed later in this chapter.

Then if your study is positive, one phase of your problem is solved. You have a printer who should do a fairly good job.

9.2.3 Using the Yellow Pages of the Phone Directory

If all else fails, use the yellow pages of the phone directory. It may not be the most fail-safe method, but as it is your only recourse, use it.

With the yellow pages, you run into the problem of selecting individuals about which you know nothing. You are basing your selection just on what is in the advertisement. It may state the truth, and then it may not. So, do some research on the particular companies you do select.

Remember, your requirements should be firmly entrenched in your mind. The printing companies should be medium-sized with the facility to do quality offset work. The particular printers should have the capacity to collate pages, bind the final manual, and perform specialized operations which might be requested. If these requirements cannot be met, disregard those printers.

9.3 DETERMINING A PRINTER'S CAPABILITIES AND MAKING A FINAL SELECTION

At this point, the field of printers has been narrowed down to a select few, whether by past experience, word of mouth, or simply through the yellow pages. The next logical step would be to make a determination of each printer's capabilities after making an initial contact.

So, set up an appointment to see each of them whether at your office or at the printing company. Preferably make the appointment at the printer's because it gives you a chance to see the company and how he or she operates. Any printer who is in business privately will be happy to have you inspect his or her shop. Of course, you will get the royal treatment as a prospective customer.

After arriving at the printer's company and exchanging pleasantries, ask for a list of his or her clients. This list is very important to you because after leaving, you can check on the printer's reputation and ability to do a good job at a fair price. If the printer has done business with any company for a long period of time, it probably is safe to assume he or she has some degree of expertise. Any company, if it is to have any reputation, must rely on its printed products to bring out the image it is trying to direct toward people. To this end, it must have a quality printer.

In line with this, ask to see samples of the work done for these companies. More than likely, the printer will want to show them to you anyway as a matter of business and pride. Even if you are a novice, you will be able to tell if the quality of the work is good or not. Check for the type of stock, whether the color is used in good taste, and if the copy is sharp and clear. These and other points can be examined and judgement passed based on common sense.

In addition, by looking at the different samples of printed work, you can get a good idea of the printer's capabilities and versatility. If you do not understand something about the work presented, ask about it. Present this same question to any of the other printers you talk with and draw your own conclusions. Any competent printer who is trying to get you as a client should be more than happy to help in this respect. This initial contact is the development of a business rapport which must be maintained during the duration of your writer/ printer relationship.

Then insist on a tour of the shop. Even though you may not know much about printing equipment, it will allow you to see how effectively the presses are utilized. Again do not be afraid to ask questions even if they may appear to be foolish. They will not be. Learn all you can at this stage of your career.

While your inspect the presses and various types of equipment, look at the shop in general. Ask yourself the following questions:

- Does the shop look dirty and disorganized?
- Do the workers look sloppy and seem to be working at a slow pace.
- Does the general work atmosphere seem unhealthy?
- Does there seem to be any resentment toward management?

By answering these questions, you can get a good idea of the general state of the printing company. First impressions, although not always right, can give you an overall picture of what type of work is produced.

Finally ask the owner what type of staff he or she has. This includes the size of the staff and the general experience of each person. In particular, see how their experience fits in with your needs as far as offset printing, color, typesetting, binding and other related skills are concerned. You should be able to make a fair judgement based on what is needed.

After your investigation of each printer is complete, go over all the facts and make your decision. If all the points have been covered, there should be no problem. When it is all over, you should have selected at least three capable printers. The selection of at least three printers is important because it provides backup for future work. In addition, three separate bids on a job assures your company of the best price for the documentation to be printed.

9.4 RECEIVING ESTIMATES ON A JOB

In the early stages of your meetings with each of the three printers, you should have initiated a good working relationship. By developing it slowly through this job and future jobs, the printer will come to know your needs and requirements. In turn, you will understand his or her capabilities and limitations. In essence, both will understand each other and learn to work easily with one another. Thus, a healthy environment will be created in which both individuals can communicate.

After selecting the three printers who will quote on your job, call them and set up an appointment, after explaining the job to be done. When each individual comes to see you, describe the job in detail so as not to waste their time. Ensure that your page count is correct, based on the typeset copy that is laid out. If possible, let them examine the artwork to give a better idea of what the job entails.

For example, if you have a manual that is broken up into six chapters, the requirements you would state to the printer might be:

- One thousand copies of the manual are to be printed and delivered by a certain date.
- The manual consists of fifty two-sided pages and six one-sided pages.
- Each chapter and the front tables begin as right-hand pages.
- The manual will be printed on 60 pound offset paper.
- The manual will be three-hole punched and inserted in three-hole binders, which will be provided.
- Six of the pages will have two colors (PMS #292 blue and black). They are 4-12, 4-13, 4-15, 4-24, 4-25 and 4-33.
- The last page (readers comments) will be standard postal weight and perforated on the left-hand side to permit removal.

Of course, as your requirements change, so will the criteria that you must dictate. In any event, place your requirements on a piece of paper and give a copy to each printer, keeping a copy for yourself. In addition, make up dummies of your manual as it is to appear in its final form. Give each printer a copy. This way, all estimates will be based on the same requirements with no deviations.

After a proper period of time, the printers should send quotes on your job. As a rule, the printers should give you a verbal quote and back it up with a binding letter. Keep the letters on file for future reference.

The question now arises as to which printer to choose. More than likely, the three quotes you have will be different. Which one should you select? First, present the figures to your immediate superior for approval, if that is the case, with your recommendations.

Remember, printing is not cheap. If you buy in quantity, the price per copy usually goes down even though the overall price is higher. The answer to this problem depends, therefore, on what quantity is needed and what management is willing to spend.

Usually the highest bid is out but not always, if you are familiar with the printer and understand the reasons. Also, you may or may not take the lowest bid, figuring the printer is trying to establish himself with your company (if this is his or her first quote). He or she may be saving money on the job in other ways which you do not know about, such as obtaining a load of inexpensive paper. The printer who gets in your company on a low bid will get his or her money back on future jobs. So, this leaves you with a middle-of-the-road quote. This is usually the one to select; however, keep an open mind and study all the facts. After using these printers once, you will get a good idea of what to expect from each and at what price.

Bear in mind that each estimate should be considered. If it is more practical to take a lower bid, by all means do it. There is no set rule. These guidelines have evolved from practical experience.

Estimates that printers make depend on labor, set-up time, cost of materials (paper), running time and any extra operations. These factors and the printer's operational size dictate the differences in estimates.

After making the selection, inform the other printers that they were not selected but will be considered for future jobs. They will appreciate this courtesy because it does not leave them hanging and they can return to their business. By doing this, you will develop a stronger writer/printer relationship with them which will be essential at a later date.

Keep everything on a business-like level in your dealings. This does not mean you cannot be friendly, but it is best if you maintain this relationship.

9.5 PREPARING A MANUAL FOR THE PRINTER

The printer's estimate has been approved and your manual is ready to be delivered to the printer. What preliminary steps must be taken to ensure that the printer receives the manual in good shape? What must the writer do to prepare the final draft copy of the manual for printing?

The printer knows, at this point, what is expected. He or she knows your specifications and how many copies must be delivered by a certain date. However, a purchase order should be made out by you on which your requirements are listed and the price quoted by the printer. This should then go through the normal purchasing cycle after being approved. The printer usually gets the original copy of the purchase order; you keep a copy, which will be filed with the appropriate quotes.

In addition to the completed purchase order, run off a copy of the manual pages again. Take these pages and assemble them as the completed manual is to appear. If the pages are two-sided, run the copy back to back. Start your chapters and front tables on right-hand pages. This dummy copy should be given to the printer who, in turn, will give it to his or her production department. If any pages have two colors, circle the appropriate areas on those pages in red ink. On the title page of the copy, indicate that a particular color is to be used on specific pages and list the page numbers.

Then take one last look through the camera-ready pages of the manual. Eliminate any dirt marks that you might run across and ensure the pages are in their proper sequence. Finally place the pages in a folder to protect them.

In addition to the camera-ready pages, gather any additional artwork that might be included. This could be art for the front and back cover, photos that might be included, etc. Put these together with the manual text.

In summary, you should have the following items for the printer:

- Completed purchase order that has been approved and processed.
- Camera-ready copy of the manual.
- Dummy copy of the manual as it is to appear.
- Any applicable artwork.

Place these items in a protective envelope carefully and seal it. Identify your company on the outside and what the envelope contains. The finished manual is now ready to be picked up by the printer. If it is prepared as indicated, the printer should have no problems.

9.6　INITIAL ASSESSMENT OF A PRINTER

The first job that is given any printer should be a test of his or her ability to do a good job in the time allotted. Your objective in this initial run will be to see how the assigned job is handled. In essence, you are testing his or her professional ability. As you give jobs out to the three printers selected over a period of time, start each one out with simple material, if possible. If the job is good, delivered on time and meets your critical standards, proceed with the next phase of your printing assessment.

When the second job is given to the printer, it should be more difficult. The printer has passed the first step, but can he or she cope with a more difficult assignment? Here again, if the job is good, delivered on time and meets your critical standards, you can be assured that he or she has that required professionalism.

More than likely, a second successful job will start building your confidence in the printer and the printer's work. If you are pleased with what you have, continue giving him or her work that is exceedingly more difficult. See if your confidence remains the same.

If the printer handles the job well and you receive your work at the time requested, you have found a true professional, an individual who is an asset to the profession. He or she provides that vital commodity, "service," on which the life of your manual depends.

9.7　LONG TERM ASSESSMENT OF A PRINTER

A printer, upon becoming a permanent fixture in a company, may tend to rest on his or her laurels, even though delivering your job professionally time and time again. This is a common occupational disease, once a printer takes a company for granted. This may not be true in all cases, but if it is, you should prepare yourself for this eventuality. If it occurs, simply sever him or her from your list of printers.

From time to time, review the various printers you use and ascertain whether their work is as good as it used to be and brings forth the company image you are trying to produce. Ask yourself the following questions:

- Do I get good cooperation from the printer every step of the way (from initial estimating to final delivery)?

- Does the printer provide the service I require? Are promises kept as far as delivery and quality of work are concerned?
- Does the typesetting and layout done by the printer contain many errors?
- Does the printer keep me informed as to problems that might arise (running late with the job, press breaking down, paper shortage, etc.)?

If the answers to these questions prove unsettling, do something about it. Remember the final responsibility for the delivery and professional quality of the manual rests with you.

9.7.1 Cooperation from the Printer

Cooperation between the printer and client is the mark of professionals. The printer should provide that cooperation that is necessary to maintain a good working relationship at all costs. The client should expect the printer to assist as far as is humanly possible. However, there is a point at which continued requests and changes border on the ridiculous.

This continued cooperation should prevail from the initial estimate of a job to its final delivery. When concern for the client's needs starts to deteriorate for no apparent reason, problems with your documentation will develop. Perhaps it will not be noticeable immediately. As you progress, however, you will notice this lack of cooperation. Watch for it.

9.7.2 Required Service

Service is a standard that all printers should maintain, but to which only the quality professionals usually adhere. It is always backed up by complete equipment, talent, experienced personnel and a compassion for the client's needs.

The printer should take that little extra time and pride in preparing your manual or other documentation. That extra amount of zeal in producing a professional piece of work is a part of such an individual. It marks him or her as a quality printer, one of a rare breed.

Service should include prompt delivery service. If a job is to be at your office on a certain date at a certain time, it should be there. If it is not, there should be a good reason, apology and some compensation. The printer is in business to make money. If he or she does not keep promises as to delivery, word will get around and the business will suffer from the bad publicity.

So, in your dealings with any printer, *insist on the service for which you pay*. If the printer is a quality professional, there should be no problem.

9.7.3 Typesetting and Layout from the Printer

You should only be concerned with this factor if your art department does not do the typesetting and layout. If the most blatant errors and shoddy workmanship occur on the final artwork from the printer on a continuing basis, bring it to his or her attention. As it progresses, insist on the necessary corrections and, possibly, sever the relationship.

There is absolutely no reason for a poor job by the printer's staff. If it happens once, mention the problem to the printer. It will be taken care of right away.

9.7.4 Problems

A mark of a concerned printer is a habit of keeping you informed of problems if they appear. Significant problems that might affect your particular job could range from the press breaking down to running late with your work. In any case, the printer should spend that extra time and money by calling and appraising you of the situation.

Another problem that might hurt you and the printer is the availability of paper. In today's economy and material shortages, paper proves to be a critical factor. Even if it can be ordered, it might be a long time in delivery. However, this problem should be known in the early stages of the printer's contact with you. At that time, the paper should have been ordered and set aside.

This trait of concern for the client by informing him or her of problems is rare. As a client, it is important to you. It helps you adjust your work schedule and gives you the opportunity to inform management of the problem.

Therefore, when the printer contacts you and informs you of problems that might occur, be grateful. It is better than not knowing at all and being surprised at the last minute.

9.8   THE FINAL PRINTING PROCESS

The finished manual is the result of modern printing technology, expertise and hard work. If quality is a key factor in producing a manual, a true printing work of art can be produced.

How then is a manual or other documentation prepared and, finally, printed? You should be aware, in general terms, of the process that is followed. Of course, you probably saw the printer's equipment and staff in your early quests for printing support, and perhaps saw a printing press in operation. There is more to the operation than this brief exposure, however. You should be aware of the entire process because you are indirectly associated with it. Knowledge of the printing process gives you a better idea of what is involved when dealing with a printer.

Normally the printer who typesets and lays out a manual has more flexibility. The printer can do the job based on his or her own needs at that particular time. As you know, job priorities change because of new requirements and additional jobs that may come in. Sometimes, one of the presses may not be available, so the job will be placed on another press. This may be done, at the time, to save money and complete your job expediently.

Prior to printing the job, the printer would send you all the camera-ready pages and related artwork before any further work is done. Any corrections or changes would be noted by you, and the camera-ready pages and artwork returned. If you had the manual typeset in your own art department, the camera-ready pages would be proofread and corrected by you before sending them to the printer.

In any case, ensure that a complete job of review and proofreading is done before any pages are sent to the printer. It is annoying to have a printer correct a page after it has been approved. A significant amount of time is lost in the operation. So, be careful. When there is a large amount of copy, it is advisable to ask for galley proofs to proof-read before camera-ready material is used to make final plates.

After camera-ready copy is received by the printer, he or she performs the following:

- Each page is photographed, making a film negative of each one. The characters on the film are checked for clarity and sharpness.
- Each negative is processed by opaquing, aligning it squarely, and placing it in the proper sequence. This process is called "stripping" by the printer. Again, the printer ensures that all characters on the film are clear and sharp.
- After all negatives have undergone the stripping process and have been aligned on large sheets, they are photomechanically burned on a sensitized plate material, that is, a source of light is shown through the film negative onto the sensitized plate surface.
- A chemical is added to the sensitized plate surface to elimi-nate the negative portions. At this point, the plate is ready to be placed on a press for use. There are different processes to stabilize plates for longer runs, as well as different types of plates for different uses.
- When the actual printing operation starts, an inked impres-sion from the plate is first made on a rubber-blanketed cyl-inder. In turn, the impression is transferred to the paper being printed. The plate never touches the paper.

NOTE: Before the final printing process, you have the final oppor-tunity to review the manual, if you desire. Ask the printer for a "blueprint" of your job. This is actually a press proof of the manual.

Of course, this is a general overview of the printing operation as it applies to you and your manual. For different requirements, different processes are involved. For example, if two colors are needed on a page, an entirely different approach is used. Basically, however, you should be aware of the offset process and printer's terminology.

9.9   FORMS OF BINDING

For your purposes in this final phase of manual production, several alternatives could be taken in presenting the final manual. Other methods of binding exist, but probably the most practical are saddle-stitching, padding, stapling, and the use of binders and dividers.

9.9.1 Saddle–Stitching

This particular process allows pages to be folded over and stapled in the centerfold as shown in Figure 9–1.

This process produces a neat looking manual with few pages, such as a small brochure or pamphlet. It is fairly popular, but has one drawback in that it cannot handle a large number of pages.

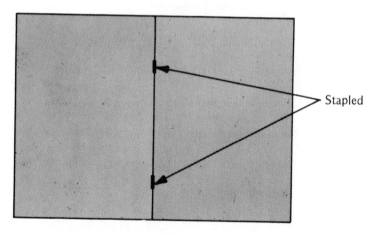

FIGURE 9-1. Saddle-Stitched Manual

9.9.2 Padded Manual

The padded process is particularly good for a user or installation manual because it can be opened fully without the manual closing back. On the left-hand edge (spine) of the front and back cover and pages,

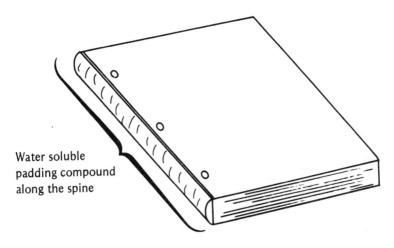

Water soluble
padding compound
along the spine

FIGURE 9-2. Padded Manual

a water soluble padding compound is applied. By using this padded concept, you tell the reader in essence that the pages are not permanent and will eventually change. Figure 9-2 illustrates a padded manual.

A variation of the padded concept is wrapping the cover around the spine of the manual, leaving a neat package. The only difference is that the pages are more permanent. It just depends on your needs and how the particular manual is to be used.

9.9.3 Stapled Manual

In the stapling process, the front and back covers and pages are collated in the proper order. Then they are stapled in two places, approximately one-quarter inch from the left-hand side of the collated manual and two inches from the top and bottom, as shown in Figure 9-3.

This process produces a neat manual but is restricted by the size of the staple. Here again, it cannot handle a large number of pages.

9.9.4 Binders and Dividers

The binder and divider concept is probably the most common approach to housing the printed pages of a manual. It is particularly

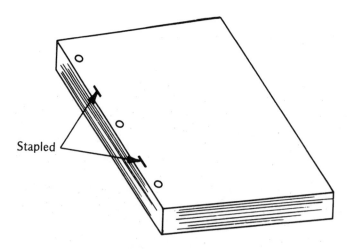

FIGURE 9-3. Stapled Manual

useful for manuals that are thick and bulky. Having three holes, the pages can be turned easily and can be taken out and inserted without any problem.

Binders can be bought as straight stock from a vendor or specially ordered with titles on the front and back covers and spine. In addition, varying ring sizes can be ordered (half-inch, one inch, inch and a half, etc.). Ensure that the rings yield sufficient room to accommodate the final printed manual.

In addition to the basic outer binder, it may be practical to use dividers before each chapter, the appendices and index of your manual. You may use them or not as you decide. If you do order them, have them preprinted on both sides of each tab with a plastic covering. In addition, have a strip of plastic running along the edge where the three holes are situated. This covering saves wear and tear on the dividers.

Normally the dividers are five-cut, which means there are five separate divider tabs from top to bottom. If more cuts are desired per set, they can be specially ordered. They may pose a problem, however, because the space provided on the tab for printing gets smaller as the number of tabs increases. If more than five tabs are required, order a set of five dividers plus the additional amount you need in a second set. For example, if there are eight chapters in a manual, order a set of five dividers and the first three of the second set of five dividers with the desired printing and plastic covering. The physical configuration of these eight, dividers is shown in Figure 9–4.

In any event, if you ordered the binders and dividers, you would work through the printer or an outside vendor. In your dealings with each, use the same principles stated throughout this chapter. Remember, demand service and quality, for your company is paying for it. Anything else is unfair to you and, in the final analysis, the reader of your manual.

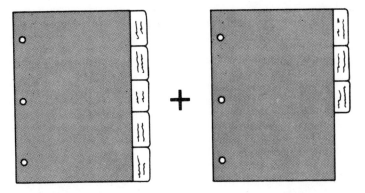

FIGURE 9–4. Physical Configuration of Eight Dividers

Index